The New
Art
of
War

China's Deep Strategy
Inside the United States

The New Art of War

China's Deep Strategy Inside the United States

William J. Holstein

Brick Tower Press
New York

Brick Tower Press
Manhanset House
Dering Harbor, New York 11965-0342
bricktower@aol.com
www.BrickTowerPress.com

Copyright © 2019 by William J. Holstein
First Edition
Library of Congress Cataloging in Publication Data
Hostein, William J.
The new art of war, china's deep strategy inside the united states.
Includes index.
1. Intelligence and Espionage—United States. 2. History of China. 3. Political Process—Media and Internet. I. Title.

ISBN: 978-1-899694-80-8

Table of Contents

Introduction...11

PART ONE: Acquiring American Technology
1   Hacking Our Secrets...25
2   Economic Espionage: Luring Chinese and
     Chinese-Americans with Secrets.......................45
3   Chinese Students and Their Systematic
     Recruitment..60
4   Buying Distressed or Undervalued American
     Companies...69
5   Venture Capital as the Entry Point..................77

 PART TWO: Shaping American Opinion and
     Decision-Making
6   Penetrating Governmental Institutions.............89
7   The Control of Opinion Platforms...................102
8   Projecting Media Power................................108
9   The Struggle for Academic Freedom...............116
10   Exporting Chinese-Style Control Systems........127
11   Playing the Game in Washington...................137

PART THREE: The Way Forward for America
12   Harden All Targets...149
13   Toward a Winning Technology Strategy..........163
14   Upskilling and Reshoring..............................178
15   Winning the "Soft War"................................189
16   Summary of Recommendations.......................201
     Acknowledgments...206
     References...207
     Index...219

PREVIOUS BOOKS

The Japanese Power Game:
What It Means for America. 1990.

Rags to Riches, the Creation of Cintas,
with Richard T. Farmer. 2002.

Manage the Media,
Don't Let the Media Manage You. 2008.

Why GM Matters:
Inside the Race to Transform An American Icon. 2009

The Next American Economy:
Blueprint For a Real Recovery, 2011.

Has the American Media Misjudged China? 2014.

How the ThinkPad Changed the World…And Is Shaping the
Future, with Arimasa Naitoh. 2017.

About the Author

Bill has been writing about the emergence of China for 40 years, ever since he was assigned as a United Press International correspondent to Hong Kong in January 1979. He won an Overseas Press Club (OPC) award for best economic coverage from abroad for his coverage of China's efforts to achieve Deng Xiaoping's economic modernization vision. The world did not know whether the Chinese could overcome the bitter ideological strife that had crippled them. Bill was the first journalist to describe how China was going to be successful in a new strategy of "getting rich," as Deng put it. As a result, Bill was promoted to become Beijing bureau chief in 1981-1982, where he studied Mandarin. He has returned many times over the years as world editor at *Business* Week, as a senior writer for *U.S. News & World Report,* and in other capacities.

While at *Business Week*, Bill guided the magazine's coverage of China as well as Japan's emergence in the late 1980s. Among many others, he wrote the 1988 cover story, *Japan's Influence in America.* Two of his books have concentrated on Japanese subjects, *The Japanese Power Game* (1990) and *How the ThinkPad Changed The World* (2017). As a former president of the OPC and current board member, in 2014 he organized a reunion of about 70 correspondents who were either currently based in Beijing or who were formerly posted there. He added his analysis and edited their remarks. The result was, *Has the American Media Misjudged China?* in late 2014. It was the first time that China-watchers sounded the alarm about Xi's presidency.

Bill added technology issues to his brief starting in 1996 when he became a senior writer for *U.S. News*. He has written about autonomous driving, big data, 3D manufacturing and other technologies that form the backdrop to U.S.-Chinese tensions.

Other news organizations he has written for include *Business 2.0, The New York Times, Fortune, Strategy & Business* and *Chief Executive*. Bill blogs on his website, williamjholstein.com and distributes his commentary on Twitter and LinkedIn. He is president of the Overseas Press Club Foundation, which helps students at American universities launch careers as foreign correspondents. It is a sister organization to the Overseas Press Club.

In short, there are few journalists today who possess the breadth of knowledge and historical perspective that Bill does in understanding America's engagement with China.

"The supreme art of war
is to subdue the enemy
without fighting."

—Sun Tzu, author, *The Art of War*

Introduction

Half a world away, Australians are engaged in a highly emotional debate about China's influence in their lives. A book by Clive Hamilton entitled, *Silent Invasion: China's Influence in Australia,* describes how the Beijing government and Communist Party are systematically attempting to influence Australian policies and cultural life. Hamilton calls it "rot at the heart of the Australian democracy."

The Australians may now understand what China is attempting to do in their country. But the Chinese government is pursuing a similar strategy in the United States and the vast majority of Americans don't understand it. If anything, the party-state's campaign in the United States is even deeper because it involves obtaining access to cutting-edge technologies, hacking massive amounts of personal information, undermining our institutions and trying to shape American perception of and policies toward China. Even in the face of President Trump's so-called trade war with China, the Chinese appear to be accelerating their efforts to penetrate American institutions and opinion-shaping bodies. This is far deeper—and systematic—than Russian efforts to polarize America through the use of social media.

Just as Clive Hamilton does in his book, I acknowledge the extreme sensitivity of these issues. What makes the debate about China's role inside America particularly sensitive is that some nearly four million Chinese-Americans are targeted by Beijing, which believes they should be loyal to it, not America.

Some Chinese-Americans and Chinese residents in the United States have cooperated in obtaining technology for the Chinese government. And many Chinese nationals who obtained years of experience working at American companies have returned to China to help competitors there. The Chinese have a nickname for these individuals, *haigui*, or returning sea turtles who come ashore once a year to lay their eggs. The challenge is to analyze and discuss the range of China's actions, some of which are entirely legitimate, without triggering hysteria or xenophobia of the sort that Senator Joseph McCarthy specialized in during the "Red Scare" of the early 1950s. A similar outburst of xenophobia earlier in history led to the Chinese Exclusion Act of 1882.

One major issue is reciprocity in the overall relationship between China and the United States today. If the Chinese government were allowing Western non-governmental organizations (NGOs) to create a stronger legal system in China, to fight for the rights of women and different nationalities within China, and to use the Internet as a tool to achieve greater political power for an emerging middle class, then we might conclude that there is a mutual process unfolding, of each country trying to learn from and shape the other.

In fact, President Xi Jinping, who has emerged with unexpected ideological intensity since taking power in 2012, is forcing NGOs to register to work with Chinese police (which subjects them to near-complete control), cracking down on dissidents and their lawyers, and turning the Internet into a tool of monitoring and repression. Simply put, he is attempting to eliminate Western ideas and establish himself as an absolute ruler for as long as he chooses. It is reminiscent of the worst type of Chinese authoritarianism, which I learned about in Beijing in the early 1980s. Xi is rallying his nation around his version of "the China dream," referring to previous eras in which China was an advanced world power. Chinese children learn about their nation's 100 years of humiliation at the hands of foreign powers who occupied large swathes of territory beginning in about 1840. The Chinese were divided among themselves as a dynasty slowly collapsed and they lacked the wealth or the technology, in the form of weapons, to resist the foreign barbarians. That period ended when Mao Tse-tung and the Communist Party won the Chinese civil war in 1949. China had "stood up." It's against that backdrop that today we see the Chinese attempting to settle historical scores and project power.

Some of the Chinese government's practices in the United States have been developing for 10 and even 20 years. It was in 1998, for example, that Joey Chun obtained Top Secret clearance from the Federal Bureau of Investigation's New York office. Starting in about 2005, he fed secrets back to China about the FBI for more than a decade before he was caught. The Central Intelligence Agency's network was compromised by a renegade former CIA agent from Hong Kong in the 2010-2011 time frame.

It appears that the full range of Chinese government actions have intensified under Xi. They have taken on a more systematic and urgent character.

Inevitably, some may feel I am displaying racism in writing this book—of being anti-Chinese. Nothing could be farther from the truth. I lived in Hong Kong and Beijing and traveled throughout much of China. I studied the Chinese language, which was the single most difficult intellectual challenge of my life. I loved China's deep history and magnificent temples. The Great Wall is truly great. I believe the Chinese possess deep wisdom as reflected in their practice of tai chi, feng shui and acupuncture, and I came to admire

Chinese art and porcelain vases long before they became fashionable. I have truly embraced the culture of China.

Moreover, I greatly admired many of the Chinese I became friends with. Their personal stories, of how they survived the Cultural Revolution, for example, were inspiring. Their determination to emerge from abject poverty has been impressive. When I first traveled in China, the cities were dark at night because they had no power. The only sound was the whir of thousands of bicycles making their way through darkened streets. What a remarkable people for having come so far since then.

But I realized over time, that there were things I didn't like about the China government—its detention camps, its silencing of dissidents, the overbearing hand of the police and security forces, and the surveillance of my communications, including a listening device in our Beijing apartment's living room. Every morning, the "listeners" would bicycle into the back gate of the diplomatic compound where my wife and I lived, Qia Jia Yuan, and go to low-slung unmarked buildings where they monitored all our communications. I knew what it felt like to live in the palm of an authoritarian government. And of course, the mass killings at Tiananmen Square in June 1989 (after I had returned to the United States), were appalling. Since returning to the United States, I have visited China approximately 20 times.

I recognized that I had to maintain a kind of neutrality, a balance, between the good and the bad. Most Westerners who grow up in the Judeo-Christian tradition of right and wrong find that difficult. In this yes-no, black-white view, the Chinese are either our friends or our enemies. But the reality is much more nuanced—they can be both. As a result, we have to learn how to manage a form of technological and economic warfare with China's government at the same time that we may cooperate on other issues. The media asks whether President Trump is trying to start a trade war or create a "new cold war." The reality is that it has already started. We just haven't recognized it as such.

Over the years, I have been a great supporter of America's engagement with China. I thought it was good for America, good for China, and good for the world. It has only been since President Xi took power that I have recognized the darker side of what China is trying to achieve in its own country—and ours. Never in my wildest dreams, or nightmares, did it occur to me that I would one day write a book about Chinese government activity in my own country. I make a distinction, by the way, between the Chinese people and the Chinese government. It is possible to admire the Chinese people but be critical of their government.

Up until the Xi presidency, it was possible to argue that China could emerge onto the world stage in a way that didn't pose a direct threat to American military or economic interests. China would accept the world order that the United States and its allies established after World War II. It certainly would not seek to interfere in our internal affairs. It would be a "responsible stakeholder" in the hopeful words of one U.S. diplomat.

But Xi has changed all that and not a single Western expert on China saw it coming. In late 2014, under the auspices of the Overseas Press Club, I organized a reunion of about 70 correspondents either currently based in Beijing or who were once posted there. It was the largest such gathering since China and the United States normalized relations. We organized four panel discussions and I edited the material for a book entitled, *Has the American Media Misjudged China? Thirty five years after China's opening to the world, some of the key assumptions that have guided coverage are being tested by the presidency of Xi Jinping.*

We were like the canary in the coal mine, the first sign of trouble. It was clear that Western news organizations, and by proxy their governments and academic experts, had failed to predict that Xi was going to steer China in a dramatically different direction than the outside world had expected. While some experts believed he was on the verge of imposing sweeping Western-style economic reforms, he surprised everyone by seeking to rebuild and revitalize the 89-million-member Communist Party and insert it into every aspect of Chinese life. He tightened control of China's Internet, securely lodged behind the Great Firewall.

He also accelerated a campaign to obtain American technology as part of the Made in China 2025 policy. The Chinese government, under the leadership of the Ministry of State Security (MSS), is coordinating digital hacks and cultivating spies in U.S. companies and government bodies. The arrest in October 2018 of a senior MSS official attempting to extract secrets from General Electric's jet engine division is a case in point. Meanwhile, China is using its economic clout to systematically snap up technologies, either through buying distressed or undervalued units of technology companies or investing in highly innovative start-ups in Silicon Valley. That's not necessarily stealing—just acquiring our best thinking for pennies on the dollar. Moreover, our open scientific research climate means Chinese researchers can find the latest discoveries in fields such as Artificial Intelligence by simply clicking on online links. They do not have to be physically present to reap the rewards of American research.

In short, if you add up all the threads, there is a massive, coordinated assault taking place on American technology, perhaps the largest, fastest transfer of intellectual property in human history, and much of it is taking place on U.S. soil. If you confront Chinese friends about this systematic pilfering in late-night drinking sessions, when truth often emerges, they will point out that China invented gunpowder, the compass and paper—and other nations stole those technologies. They also point out that the United States stole technology from Britain; such as the steam engine. So if we Americans did it, we're being hypocritical in saying the Chinese don't have a right to do the same thing. That's why the Chinese cannot be persuaded to stop—they have convinced themselves it is their right to do so. If we are naive enough to leave ourselves vulnerable, they will take advantage of that weakness. That's entirely fair in much of Chinese culture. The question is whether we have the will to recognize the pattern and stop it.

It's not just some abstract technologies at stake. Developing and manufacturing high-tech goods creates tens of thousands of the kind of high-skilled, high-paying jobs that every nation wants. If we lose control of the development of a technology, we also lose the possible jobs that go with it.

Elsewhere, our governmental institutions have been under assault. The FBI revealed in 2017 that Joey Chun had been feeding secrets about the agency's technology and surveillance practices for such a long period of time. That almost certainly weakened the FBI's ability to detect Chinese operatives—although the FBI was able to recently break up an apparent plan to insert a mole into the U.S. Army.

Moreover, the Chinese army may have succeeded in planting chips on the servers used by the U.S. Navy, both houses of Congress, and the Department of Homeland Security that give them a "trapdoor," or a way to control them, according to *Bloomberg BusinessWeek*. Chinese hackers have repeatedly targeted the U.S. Navy, seeking not only technological secrets but also mundane details such as ship maintenance data and lists of 100,000 naval personnel with their names, birthdays, Social Security numbers and cell phone numbers.

Hacking groups that either work directly for the Chinese government or are affiliated with it have conducted massive penetrations of U.S. computer systems, seizing nearly 400 million personal records from the Marriott Hotel group and 22 million records of U.S. government employees from the Office of Personnel Management. The thievery does not appear to be taking place for commercial gain. Experts believe the Chinese party-state is attempting to use the data to prevent U.S. agencies from planting their own spies in China and to identify travel patterns of dissidents and other critics in the United States.

At the same time, the Chinese government is seeking to manage the American debate about China by creating new opinion platforms, denying visas to professors who do not adhere to the party-state's line, spending millions on projecting soft power and intimidating Hollywood studios into making movies that will please Chinese censors and therefore be shown in China as well as other markets.

Many nations seek to obtain American technology and seek to influence American perceptions and decision-making. But the sheer scale and ambition of what China is doing is more significant because the United States and China are the world's two largest economies and China, under Xi, is clearly seeking to upstage the United States and create its own world order based on Chinese interests.

It seems clear now that China's emergence under one-man authoritarian rule is the greatest challenge the United States has faced since World War II—larger even than the Soviet threat, which ultimately crumbled, and larger than Islamic terrorism, which is much less complex than the multi-dimensional challenge the Chinese government is posing. The party-state is clearly utilizing the size of its population—1.4 billion versus 327 million people in the United States—as an advantage.

Americans might be forgiven for not being terribly interested in what China is doing in South Africa or South Asia. But certainly Americans have a vital stake in what China is doing in our own country. That's why the China challenge on our own territory is so dangerous—we have not recognized it. Nor, in the present state of a seemingly permanent social and political divide in our society, is it certain that we will be able to agree on a response.

Our goal should not be preventing China from emerging on the world stage. It is their right to develop on their own steam. But we need to make sure that we retain leadership in at least some critical technologies. One obvious reason is that technologies such as Artificial Intelligence (AI) have clear military uses. But more broadly, if we have to rely on others for advanced products, that creates a measure of dependency. If the Chinese sell us AI systems and we sell them only soybeans, that tilts the balance of power and unacceptably so. And we certainly need to maintain the integrity of the institutions that make up the American democracy.

Both Trump and Vice President Mike Pence have suggested that China's actions are aimed at defeating Trump at the ballot box. They hope to deflect attention from Russia's involvement in the 2016 election. I am not involved in any political gamesmanship. I have no dog in that hunt. I am simply documenting that the Chinese government's actions are much deeper, longer-term and more strategic than Russia's. Judging by their actions, they seek to extract the technology necessary to give China parity with the United States or outright dominance and to prevent our institutions from either recognizing the challenge or mounting an effective defense.

Each of the strategies that I will discuss in this book could have appeared in the ancient Chinese text, *The Art of War*, which discussed the psychological and perceptual issues that affect the outcomes of great battles. That book dates to the Warring States era from the 5th Century B.C. to the 3rd Century B.C. The Chinese have been skilled strategists and warriors long before European civilization developed.

For the record, the Chinese government routinely and consistently denies that it interferes in the internal affairs of other sovereign nations or engages in cyber attacks—positions that simply do not square with the facts I will present in this book.

The challenge today is this: how can America's fractured democracy and diverse society respond to a centrally orchestrated strategy from China on our own soil that challenges our interests and our values? I will provide answers in my final chapters, no matter how unpopular and complex they may be. We need a structural response, not rhetorical flourishes. The first step is hardening our technology targets and government institutions while at the same time opening up the valves of innovation even further. We need to do a better job of training and retraining, which is connected to our ability to bring at least some jobs home. And politically, we must define a new center to concentrate on issues where broad American agreement is possible rather than dwelling exclusively on the issues that divide us.

Throughout this book, I have used my own research but also material from news organizations. This has been deliberate, not an act of intellectual sloth. I wanted to show that the facts presented in this book are more than the fertile imagination of one author. Further, the reality is that no single writer would be able to establish expertise and contacts in Hollywood, Silicon Valley, immigration enforcement, universities, intelligence agencies, business and the media. They are different universes unto themselves, which is one reason Americans have been slow to understand the pattern of how Chinese efforts in each sector fit together.

Similarly, different arms of the U.S. government have described different pieces of the Chinese government's strategy, as have academic studies. Court documents contain a treasure trove of insight and detail. The experts have been talking to other experts, but no one has told the people. What has been missing is the effort to add up the facts and assemble them into a coherent and comprehensible whole, which is what this book represents.

The reader may fairly ask about my political persuasions. I consider myself a radical centrist who wants to focus on what I think are the big economic and technological challenges we as a nation face. I also accept the label of being an "economic patriot." I think the term "nationalist" is too harsh because it implies a willingness to run roughshod over the interests of others. But I want America to win in the world, and at home, by doing what it does best—rallying around common causes.

A note on Chinese names: there is no way to consistently present Chinese names in English. In Chinese, the family name comes first followed by given names. So it is Xi Jinping. Some Chinese, seeking to appear more Westernized, reverse the order. So the name becomes Jinping Xi. Others have adopted Western given names, making it Joseph Xi. I have used the style of name that given Chinese individuals have chosen to present to the world or that U.S. agencies have presented rather than trying to impose consistency. I have also used the term "party-state" because the Communist Party and the Chinese government have been effectively merged under Xi. Under him, the state is the party and the party is the state.

There are five types of spies to be employed:

"Local spies—employ people from the local district.
"Internal spies—employ their people who hold
    government positions.
"Double agents—employ the enemy's spies.
"Expendable spies—are employed to spread
    disinformation outside the state. Provide our
    (expendable) spies (with false information) and
    have them leak it to enemy agents.
"Living spies—return with their reports.

"Thus the highest realization of warfare is to attack
    the enemy's plans; next is to attack their
    alliances; next to attack their army; and the
    lowest is to attack their fortified cities."

—Sun Tzu, author, *The Art of War*

PART ONE

Acquiring American Technology

"A skilled attack is
one against which opponents
do not know how to defend."

—Zhuge Liang, Chinese politician
and military strategist (181-234 A.D)
and *Art of War* commentator

1 Hacking Our Secrets

The chief information officer of a mid-sized Midwest manufacturing company was out playing golf one sunny Saturday morning when his boss, the company's chief executive officer, called him on his cell phone. The CEO was angry because he was having problems with the company email account. "This was everyone's worst nightmare," the chief information officer told me.

The CIO, whom I interviewed for a *Chief Executive* article in 2016[1] (and whose identity I pledged to protect), checked the company's Information Technology systems, using his cell phone. The company had a separate email server, or computer, connected to the Internet and it was sending out enormous streams of data—on a Saturday when few employees were working—which was why the CEO has having trouble using it. "We didn't know what was going on for a couple of days until we looked at where the traffic was going," he told me. "All of it was going to one location in Shanghai and we didn't have any customers or operations there. The information being targeted was export control documents we had filed with the U.S. government to export equipment to the United Kingdom, India and Spain." The company supplies Boeing, Airbus, Lockheed Martin—and the U.S. Navy.

It turns out the hackers were attempting to obtain confidential information about the parts purchased by the U.S. Navy. "We were told by FireEye (a major Internet security company) that the attack was similar to other attacks by a unit of the People's Liberation Army called simply, Unit 61398. They had been tracking these guys and knew their patterns."

When most Americans hear about Chinese attempts to steal or otherwise obtain U.S. technology, they assume it is a problem facing big companies operating in China. They might not think it's a problem here. As has been widely reported, American firms in China are under pressure to create joint ventures with Chinese state-owned or state-backed enterprises, who seek to absorb the American technology over a period of time. The end goal, the Chinese have announced in their Made in China 2025 program and other five-year plans, is that they want to be independent—and perhaps dominant—in key technologies such as AI, semiconductors, autonomous driving, drones, 5G wireless networks (which will be as much as 100 times faster than today's networks), quantum computing, supercomputers, genetic editing and other cutting edge fields by that year.

But the pressures on big companies in China is only one piece of the equation. The Chinese have reached the point of sophistication that they understand which small and medium-sized companies supply parts to the U.S. defense sector. Large defense contractors such as Northrup Grumman, Lockheed Martin and General Dynamics are harder targets because if they detect a threat, they share the information with the Pentagon. If the Pentagon perceives a threat, it shares it with its major contractors. The system acts as a kind of cyber shield. But assuming they would never be targets, many smaller suppliers have not erected sufficient defenses against hackers. Not only can Chinese hackers get into the systems of these smaller companies, they can use those company's systems as subterfuge to penetrate the larger companies. Because companies these days are linked electronically through their supply chains, and will be increasingly linked as the world moves toward the Internet of Things, an electronic approach to Raytheon, say, from a smaller supplier would not necessarily trigger alarm bells because the supplier is seen as friend, not foe.

The overall campaign against America's technology secrets is clearly coordinated and massive in scale. It also involves enticing Chinese or Chinese-American employees of American companies inside the United States to steal certain types of secrets. It involves recruiting Chinese employees and Chinese students back to China with generous job offers if they bring certain know-how. They are routinely offered triple their current salaries. Because the Chinese are cash-rich, the campaign to target U.S. technologies in America also includes the purchase of faltering divisions of high-tech companies or smaller technology companies, and the use of venture capital to secure windows of access into highly innovative firms.

No one knows precisely how many companies have been hacked by the Chinese but the suspicion is that it is commonplace, particularly in the so-called "dual use" sector, meaning companies that make products used for both commercial and military purposes. An agreement in September 2015 between then-President Obama and Chinese President Xi[2] led to a dramatic decline in the number of attacks on U.S. companies whose products are purely for commercial use. But the cyber hacks against smaller and medium-sized U.S. dual use manufacturers have continued unabated—in some cases with renewed ferocity. Smaller suppliers have been the rich underbelly of the American defense industry.

The Midwest manufacturing company was smart enough to call in the experts at FireEye when it detected the trail leading to Shanghai. "We discovered that the Chinese had been in our systems for two months before we found them," the CIO told me. "The forensics work showed that they did a lot of poking around and knew what they were looking for.

They had set up a process for getting the data out by compressing the files so they could be exfiltrated."

The investigators believe Unit 61398 had been able to get into the company's systems by sending a phishing email that an employee clicked on. That was all it took.

FireEye helped the company stop the attack before the hackers could obtain any sensitive information. "We stopped them manually in mid-exfiltration and they couldn't get back in," the CIO recalls. "Which meant they did not have time to clean up and cover their tracks. We could see all the trails they had left. Our whole directory of emails and passwords had been compromised. They had taken a lot of documents and Requests-For-Proposals (RFPs), but they had not yet taken our drawings, which are the secret sauce. If they had gone for the drawings first, it would have been better for them."

Cleaning up and making sure it couldn't happen next took time and money. "We had to do things like check all the software in our servers to make sure we had current versions and therefore there were no vulnerabilities. We had eight different locations around the world where we had a connection to the Internet. Think of that like having eight doors into your house that someone could get in through."

The company had to change every employee's password and take other remediation steps. Surprisingly, Unit 61398 kept trying to get back into the company's systems. "The Chinese tried three more times after that episode to get back in," the CIO said. "After a while, this sort of thing starts to piss you off."

What makes it hard to defend against Chinese hackers is that they adopt a very long-term view and are willing to infect a target company's systems and wait years for the company to develop useful secrets. The thieves may insert malware, which means malicious software aimed at doing harm, that is dormant in a system until it is activated years later. The malicious software can even work its way up through different levels of a company's system until it is accepted as legitimate. Malware comes in different forms—viruses, worms and Trojans are some of the terms used to describe it.

FireEye, which attempts to protect its customers' networks around the world, says it tracks more than 20 entities in China, called "threat groups," that hack into other nations' Information Technology (IT) systems to obtain secrets. Christopher Porter, chief intelligence strategist at FireEye and a former employee of the U.S. Central Intelligence Agency (CIA), told me that some of the groups are affiliated with the military and others with universities.

But there is little doubt that they are coordinated by the Chinese party-state. What helps establish that is a simple fact—after the Obama-Xi agreement, the decline in attacks on commercial targets was precipitous. "There certainly was some kind of edict that came down that said Beijing wanted everyone in the country to comply with this diplomatic agreement," Porter explains. "I'm very confident that the Chinese government has complied with the thrust of the agreement as they said they would—it's just that's a very narrow norm." Even threat groups not affiliated with the government, which act as "freelancers," appeared to cease their attacks on commercial targets within a matter of months.

In the defense and dual-use areas, however, "the threat has always been high and that hasn't changed at all," Porter adds. "Defense contractors are targeted all the time."

The Chinese are going after companies that make semiconductors and satellite navigational gear, for example, even if they sell only small portions of their products to the military. That's what the term "dual use" means.

Then there are other fields not covered by the Obama-Xi agreement, such as cloud computing networks managed by large technology companies. "The Chinese are still engaged in a lot of activity you want to stop," Porter said. "They are stealing millions of healthcare records from hospitals. They are still collecting information for business negotiation purposes, wanting to know what price a U.S. board of directors may pay to buy out a company somewhere in the world. And they want to know about the bids that U.S. companies are putting in on international projects." The obvious reason is that Chinese companies may want to buy the same companies and bid on the same projects. No one knows why China's hackers are stealing healthcare records.

Even if it can't pinpoint a geographic location for a Chinese threat group, FireEye assembles a portrait of the entity by studying what tools and what electronic infrastructure it uses. "We also look at the victims," Porter added. "This is inferential. If we look at a group that is targeting East Asia and Southeast Asia looking for political information and is also stealing intellectual property from the United States, and if it has certain tactical characteristics, we can assume they are Chinese."

The Chinese threat groups have been clever because they have not attempted any denial-of-service attacks that crash a company's systems and they haven't been as brash as North Korea was when it targeted Sony's Hollywood operations because of an unflattering movie about leader Kim Jung-Un. "The Chinese do damage to many companies but not major damage to any one company," Porter said. "That's how they have kept it off the White House agenda."

The United States Trade Representative's Office, in a little noticed 215-page complaint in March 2018[3], argued that China's cyber intrusions match up neatly with the goals it has articulated in its various five-year plans for different technologies.

Porter said it's important to understand the cyber attacks as part of a larger strategy. When Chinese officials or partners approach a U.S. company in China and demand a particular technology, somehow they have learned precisely what to ask for. That knowledge could have come from their cyber campaign. The Chinese also are employing human means in the United States to get access to the technologies they want, as demonstrated in Chapter Two. "Part of why I'm so confident that commercial intellectual property theft is down is because of the success of these other means of getting it," he said.

American military and intelligence hackers are doubtlessly probing and monitoring Chinese systems but it seems clear that American hacking in China is small in comparison with the waves of Chinese hacking in America. The language barrier is part of the explanation—the Chinese possess far more English-speakers than the United States possess Chinese-speakers, even when adjusted for relative population sizes. And then there is the issue of numbers—with a population of 1.4 billion—the Chinese can train and deploy far more hackers and electronic experts than the United States can train and deploy defenders. The country has 800 million people who use the Internet, most often with their smart phones, suggesting a huge pool of tech-savvy operators[4]. They can, it turns out, reach into systems even in the tranquil green fields of the American Midwest.

* * *

Just months after I spoke with Porter, the APT10 case broke. Deputy Attorney General Rod J. Rosenstein and FBI Director Chris Wray, in late December 2018, announced that a grand jury in the Southern District of New York had indicted two Chinese nationals in Tianjin, a coastal city near Beijing[5]. Zhu Hua and Zhang Shilong, who had a number of colorful aliases such as "Godkiller," both worked for Huaying Haitai Science and Technology Development Company and acted in association with the MSS's Tianjin branch, the indictment alleged[6]. They were known to Western cyber security companies as the APT10 group, with APT standing for "Advanced Persistent Threat."

APT10 launched two different campaigns. The first one was identified as a "technology theft campaign" and it started in about 2006. Just like Unit 61398 did in the case of the Midwest manufacturer supplying the U.S. Navy, APT10 started out with phishing messages that were customized to the individuals to whom they were sent. To trick recipients into opening the attachments, the emails purported to originate from legitimate sources, when in fact they were originating from APT10.

What APT10 got away with was astonishing. It got into the computers of 45 entities in at least 12 states, including Arizona, California, Connecticut, Florida, Maryland, New York, Ohio, Pennsylvania, Texas, Utah, Virginia and Wisconsin. Victim companies included those in aviation, space and satellite technology, manufacturing, pharmaceutical, oil and gas exploration and production, communications, computer processors and maritime technologies. No one attempted to put a price tag on the value of the technology but it must have been in the billions of dollars. None of the companies were identified. It is not clear when the Technology Theft Campaign ended.

Then in 2014—before Xi signed the agreement with Obama not to engage in hacking for commercial purposes—APT10 started its campaign to target what Rosenstein called Managed Service Providers (MSPs). These are more popularly known as cloud computing service providers. They include IBM, Microsoft, Amazon Web Services and the like. The big service providers have convinced hundreds of corporate customers and government agencies to use the server farms that the big IT companies have built to store data and get access to software or other services they may need. It's cheaper than doing it all themselves. In the early days of this shift to cloud computing, companies said they were worried that their secrets would be more exposed if their data were off their own premises in a facility managed by someone else. But the cloud providers prevailed by arguing that company data would be more protected because the big IT providers had more specialized security knowledge and full-time staff dedicated to preventing breaches. APT10 and its "MSP Theft Campaign" proved the best minds in American technology could be beaten over a period of four years.

Over time, APT10's techniques and tradecraft grew in sophistication. Once a recipient opened an email attachment, it installed malware on the victim's computer. The malware typically included customized versions of a Remote Access Trojan, or RAT, which allowed the computers to be controlled remotely. They also downloaded keystroke logging malware into the host systems, which allowed them to steal usernames and passwords as a legitimate user typed them in. If the hackers could log in as legitimate users, they were going to be very difficult to stop.

APT10 also developed a system that kept shifting their domain names so that anyone monitoring the big cloud computing systems would not notice that a particular user was sending enormous numbers of emails back and forth. As I understand it, a domain name is like "tianjinhacking.com." If the hackers used that name, it would have set off alarms and if they used any domain name too often, that also could raise concerns about why such a large volume of email was going to one address. "The APT10 group used dynamic Domain Name System service providers to host their malicious domains," the indictment said. That "allowed the APT10 Group to route the pre-programmed malicious domains in their malware to different addresses of computers under their control." That also bypassed network security filters that might block malicious-sounding addresses. When they had complete control of the cloud computing servers, they were able to leapfrog horizontally into the systems of customer companies. They were virtually invisible. Ultimately, when they identified information they wanted, they made copies of files in encrypted archives and exfiltrated them.

Through this campaign, APT10 compromised the cloud networks of the big IT providers and penetrated clients located in at least 12 countries, including Brazil, Canada, Finland, France, Germany, India, Japan, Sweden, Switzerland, the United Arab Emirates, the United Kingdom and the United States. The companies were engaged in banking and finance, telecommunications and consumer electronics, medical equipment, packaging, manufacturing, consulting, healthcare, biotechnology, automotive, oil and gas exploration, and mining.

Some of APT10's efforts had a strategic intent: it compromised more than 40 computers to steal confidential data from the U.S. Navy, including personally identifiable information of more than 100,000 personnel. That included names, Social Security numbers, dates of birth, salary information, personal phone numbers and email addresses.

The Wall Street Journal identified one of the cloud services companies as IBM, which told the newspaper it had seen no evidence that sensitive company or client data had been compromised.[7] Presumably, that is because APT10 made copies of everything it stole and was able to cover its tracks before investigators could detect its presence. IBM did not respond to my request for comment.

FireEye says it knew about APT10 for years before the U.S. government took action. It's not clear what precipitated the crackdown. FireEye's Porter said it could have been a change in internal politics in America—officials in the U.S. security and intelligence agencies finally decided it was time to strike a blow. "Targeting an MSP does not violate the Xi agreement the way it was interpreted under Obama and the first year of the Trump Administration—it's the interpretation that has changed, not China's behavior," Porter told me.

Whatever triggered the American decision to crack down on the APT10 operation, it required an extraordinary degree of cooperation among different organizations all across the United States to stop it. The FBI's offices in New Orleans, New Haven, Houston, New York, Sacramento and San Antonio were involved. The Pentagon's Defense Criminal Investigative Service (DCIS) and the U.S. Naval Criminal Investigative Service (NCIS) cooperated, as did the Justice Department's National Security Division's Counterintelligence and Export Control Section. It took that much firepower to unravel what APT10 had achieved.[8] The indictment offered a back-handed compliment to APT10, saying it had demonstrated "advances in overcoming network defenses, victim selection, and tradecraft."

Both Rosenstein and Wray delivered very pointed messages in a televised press conference, with large signs behind them showing pictures of the two Chinese hackers and proclaiming "Wanted by the FBI: APT10 Group." The U.S. officials said what China was doing was "unacceptable" and "galling. "No country should be able to flout the rule of law— so we're going to keep calling out this behavior for what it is: illegal, unethical, and unfair," Wray said.

Clearly, the Xi-Obama agreement of 2015 had taken a beating. Joseph S. Campbell, who spent 25 years at the FBI, rising to become assistant director of its Criminal Investigative Division, told me that the APT10 compromise of America's cloud computing infrastructure had "just a really devastating impact."

Campbell, who worked on white collar and organized crime, cyber crime, weapons of mass destruction, drug dealing, anti-terrorism and civil rights, is now a director in the global Investigations and Compliance practice at Navigant Consulting, based in Washington, D.C. "You have to look at it from the perspective of the government of China and their strategy as a whole, which is to become the preeminent superpower, eclipsing the U.S., and having significant impact globally," he said.

"What it shows is how effective the Chinese government has been, as a one-party authoritarian state, at using all its resources in the military, in its intelligence apparatus, in its businesses and in its academic sector, working with the (Chinese) diaspora located around the world, to develop these strategies to target areas like cloud computing and other technology," he added.

Having been involved in fighting cyber-hacking, Campbell knows a bit more about the precise methods APT10 and other hacking groups use than disclosed in the indictment. "The Chinese and others in some cases have developed or enhanced malware that disguises itself as legitimate software systems," he explained. "It tricks the target's intrusion detection and prevention systems, and allows those viruses then to enter. And then often they are immediately transferred to other networks. They also can be introduced through third party vendors, who have weak or non-existent systems or systems that can be easily compromised. Then they will hop to other systems to identify what is most lucrative to target."

The hackers have plenty of time to conduct surveillance because they are essentially invisible. They look for users who are engaged in work that might be of interest to the Chinese government. "They use a lot of phishing techniques," Campbell said. "Over time, they are able to study the habits, speech patterns and typing patterns of individuals within a corporation and use that information to send what appear to be legitimate emails to other individuals in the company or other businesses they are working with. They can trick them into clicking on links or providing information that is sensitive, and as a means to steal product and money. The Chinese have obviously gone to great lengths to perfect their methodologies."

None of the impassioned rhetoric from America's top law enforcement officials is likely to dissuade the Chinese from continuing the attacks. In something akin to a nuclear arms race, they just keep striving to become more sophisticated.

* * *

Another piece of the Chinese government's effort to deeply penetrate American computer systems was the stunning revelation in *Bloomberg BusinessWeek* in October 2018[9] that the People's Liberation Army (PLA), which is China's military, had forced subcontractors in China to install a tiny chip the size of a grain of rice onto thousands of servers, which are the building blocks of many advanced computing systems in the United

States. These tiny chips are relatively simple but they enable the PLA to take control of any computer system where they are present. That means all the software and data in that system is visible to the PLA.

BusinessWeek, which conducted 100 interviews over the course of a year, described how Amazon.com in 2015 was trying to decide whether to buy a Portland, Ore.-based company called Elemental Technologies. It made software for compressing massive video files such as the kind the Central Intelligence Agency obtains from drones. Elemental used servers designed by Super Micro Computer Inc., which is based in San Jose, Ca. and is commonly called Supermicro. It is the one of the world's largest suppliers of servers, which are the brains, so to speak, of all computing systems. Supermicro handled all the engineering for its servers but sourced the components, such as the motherboards, from different manufacturers in China. By some estimates, China makes 75 percent of the world's mobile phones and 90 percent of its personal computers.

Amazon grew suspicious about Elemental's security and hired an independent third-party company to take apart Supermicro's server motherboards being used with Elemental's software. There they found the tiny PLA chip that was not part of the original design. Amazon reported the discovery to U.S. authorities, who were able to learn that officials from the PLA had approached Supermicro's supplier in China and succeeded in persuading it to install the tiny bugs.

BusinessWeek said the computing systems of at least 30 American companies were affected, including Apple. Both Amazon and Apple vehemently denied that they had discovered any Trojan Horse-style implants. The U.S. government remained largely silent on the case but a top-secret investigation is continuing, the magazine said. No other news organization could match the *BusinessWeek* reporting because of the amount of time and access that was required.

Elemental's computers were also used extensively in the U.S. government and the CIA had even invested in the company through its venture capital arm. Public documents showed that its servers had been used inside Department of Defense data centers to process drone and surveillance-camera footage, on Navy warships to transmit feeds of airborne missions, and inside government buildings to enable secure videoconferencing. NASA, both houses of Congress and the Department of Homeland Security also have been customers, according to the magazine.

Supermicro is run by a Taiwanese native who was educated in the United States and it employs both Taiwanese and mainland engineers. The dominant language spoken is Mandarin, which might have made it easier for the PLA to figure out its designs and how to implant the chips. There is no hint that Supermicro itself knew about the secret chip.

The chip was capable of telling the computing system to communicate with one of several anonymous computers elsewhere on the Internet and preparing the device's operating system to accept code from the anonymous computers, which were presumably controlled by the PLA. In short, the PLA could exert complete control.

Do the Chinese army and party-state possess the necessary skills to pull off such a penetration? "Of course, China is capable of doing it," Andrew J. Grotto, who served on the National Security Council (NSC) within the White House in both the Obama and Trump administrations, told me. He was senior director for cybersecurity policy, putting him at the heart of the government's efforts to come to grips with cybercrime. He is now a fellow at Stanford University in California.

Grotto has no knowledge of whether the PLA did it, only that the Chinese would be capable of it, based on his understanding of their technological strengths. I believe it happened. Having worked at *BusinessWeek* for 11 years, I understand the care and effort that go into major cover stories. The magazine could not possibly have simply fabricated the story. There are too many internal checks and balances, too many editors, fact-checkers and lawyers.

The implications are staggering. One is that the PLA can monitor not only commercial and technological activity in the West but also might have the capability of watching the U.S. Navy's air operations remotely, which could provide a military advantage if ever acted upon. It does not appear the chips have been activated as yet. The PLA checks in every once in a while with its secret chips but does not appear to have started a massive pilfering of data, the magazine said.

A major question is what U.S. companies and governmental bodies can or will do about this reported penetration as well as others. Companies routinely deny many hacking reports that do not involve customer information because they fear negative reactions from shareholders, the U.S. government, customers and other constituencies. One constituency they also don't want to offend by making a public stink—the Chinese government—particularly if they have large sales in China, as Apple certainly does. These companies *must* deny. That is the only viable short-term option.

Because of the sensitivity of the issues, no outsiders know exactly what American companies and institutions are doing in response to the discovery of the PLA chip. "Over the decades, the security of the supply chain became an article of faith despite repeated warnings by Western officials," the magazine wrote. "A belief formed that China was unlikely to jeopardize its position as workshop to the world by letting its spies meddle in its factories. That left the decision about where to build commercial systems resting largely on where capacity was greatest and cheapest. 'You end up with a classic Satan's bargain,' one former U.S. official says. 'You can have less supply than you want and guarantee it's secure, or you can have the supply you need, but there will be risk. Every organization has accepted the second proposition." In other words, companies are using computer equipment they know could be potentially risky but it is cheap and therefore more profitable than trying to build the equipment in the United States or in another secure setting.

One expert who takes a dim view of the U.S. corporate and governmental response to all forms of Chinese government hacking is Steve Mancini, who spent three years at the Department of Homeland Security's National Cybersecurity and Communications Center, a 24-hour, 7-day a week office that coordinates the entire federal government's strategy against intrusions into its systems. Now an adjunct professor at Seton Hill University in southwestern Pennsylvania, Mancini assists in forensic investigations of many different forms of cybercrime.

"We're a mess," Mancini told me. "The theft of intellectual property has been going on for at least 15 years. Strategically, China is a country absolutely hell-bent on regaining what it thinks is its rightful place as the center of the universe. They have thousands of years of history. They don't think in terms of days, weeks, or months, even years. They think in terms of decades and decades."

He said major defense contractors are starting to respond to the Federal Acquisition Regulation (FAR), which requires better security measures for sub-contractors. "Does that mean our supply chain is safe? Absolutely not," he said. "Is it really being made in the United States or is it being outsourced to China somewhere far down the supply chain? Think about IT hardware. Do we read the label to see where the equipment is made? No. And if the work is being done in the United States, there's a good chance it is being done by foreign nationals on H1B visas. In fact, it's been reported that more than 70 percent of Silicon Valley's tech workforce are foreign nationals."[10]

Mancini agrees with other intelligence experts that the technology-grabbing efforts are coordinated by the Chinese government. "I don't see how it could *not* be coordinated," he said. "Where is the stolen information going? It's going to Chinese companies for two reasons. For one, it's helping them build their infrastructure. If I steal a bunch of information from Westinghouse about nuclear power plants, I can build them at home without spending money on R&D. Secondly, I can have my nation-state-backed companies build them for other markets and again they don't spend millions of dollars on R&D. I think it's a disaster. We're not doing anything about it."

He makes a very serious accusation—at least some American companies are using computer systems they know might be compromised but decline to involve the U.S. government in attacking the problem. "Large U.S. corporations are making a lot of money in China," Mancini added. "Do you think they want to interrupt this cash stream? I can crank out smart phones in China at rock bottom prices because I don't have to worry about labor laws or environmental laws. If I don't worry about those things, I can make these things for cheap and bring them into the West and sell them for $1,200. Why do you think these smart phone companies are worth so much?

"The U.S. government has no reason to change things because industry isn't crying yet. If you're making money in

China because of lower manufacturing costs, the last thing you want is our government pushing back against a country where your goods are being manufactured and you're charging customers four or five times what it cost to make them.. You're not going to upset the apple cart."

If he's right, it's a classic case of a country hooked on tweets and short-term tactical thinking, based in part on quarterly earnings reports and the latest political polls, confronting a party-state that thinks primarily about its long-term strategic interests.

* * *

Aside from stealing data, Chinese state-backed companies may be seeking to monitor some key Americans. *The Washington Post* reported in January 2019 that opposition had developed to the District of Columbia's consideration of a Chinese company as the provider of new subway cars for an upgrade of the Metro mass transit system.[11] "The warnings sound like the plot of a Hollywood spy thriller," reporters Robert McCartney and Faiz Siddiqui wrote. "The Chinese hide malware in a Metro rail car's security camera system that allows surveillance of Pentagon or White House officials as they ride the Blue Line—sending images back to Beijing."

The China Railway Rolling Stock Corp. (CRRC) has won four of five large U.S. transit rail car contracts awarded since 2014—in Boston, Chicago, Los Angeles and Philadelphia. Washington's Metro system is expected to spend more than $1 billion for at least 256 new rail cars. In other bidding contests, CRRC has been able to undercut competitors on the basis of price, often by hundreds of millions of dollars. Part of the opposition to CRRC is that China is attempting to dominate the rail car industry as part of its Made in China 2025 plan.

But another set of concerns revolves around the possibility that security cameras in the rail cars could track government workers and possibly listen to their conversations. Grotto, the former NSC cyber guru, wrote online that the District of Columbia should insert clear language in its Request for Proposals that all security camera gear be screened by an independent third party to make sure it is secure. "The risk of espionage is uniquely high in our nation's capital," Grotto said. "Malware could divert data collected from the high definition security cameras. An adversary with that data could then use facial recognition algorithms to track riders, potentially right down to the commuting patterns of individual riders."

Congress, the Pentagon and industry experts have prevailed on the Metro system to rewrite its RFP to make it clear that the security camera systems in the rail cars will be thoroughly vetted. As outlandish and as paranoid as the critics may seem, the technological capabilities described by Grotto are well within the Chinese government's reach because it has been rolling out cameras and facial recognition systems all over its own country.

2 Economic Espionage: Luring Chinese and Chinese-Americans at U.S. Companies with Secrets

In August 2018, the FBI arrested a General Electric engineer named Xiaoqing Zheng, who was born in China and had Chinese citizenship, but who also had U.S. citizenship. Prosecutors said Zheng, who lived with his family in Niskayuna, N.Y, near Albany, had used very sophisticated means to remove electronic files from GE's turbine division. He encrypted the files with a type of software the company did not use, which is what triggered suspicion. He concealed the files in a picture of a sunset and sent it to his private HotMail account.[1]

Zheng, who went to college in the United States and who had worked for GE since 2008, told prosecutors he and his brothers owned a technology firm in Nanjing, China, that supplies parts for civil aviation engines. Investigators learned that he was working for several different aviation technology companies in China, including some funded by the Chinese government. His intent was clear.

Here's one telling aspect of the arrest: FBI agents who searched his home found a handbook that described the resources that China's government provides to individuals who obtain certain technologies. In other words, an unidentified arm of the Chinese government—presumably the Ministry of State Security (MSS)—had created a list of what technologies it wants Chinese and Chinese-Americans working at U.S. companies in the United States to obtain or steal. The GE incident was not a random event. It was part of a consciously crafted strategy. The MSS, according to FBI court documents, has responsibilities for civilian intelligence inside China, foreign intelligence and counter-intelligence, giving it broader responsibilities than either the FBI or CIA.

Chinese and Chinese-Americans make enormous contributions to America's technology sector. I've been deep inside the research labs at Carnegie Mellon and the Massachusetts Institute of Technology and also deep into the R&D labs of such companies as IBM, Medtronic and Corning. Almost without exception, Chinese or Chinese-Americans are present, as well as many other nationalities and cultures. It's part of the secret of what makes the United States such an innovative nation—we allow and encourage a variety of national and cultural perspectives to come together to solve problems. One Chinese-American, An Wang, helped give birth to the personal computer industry by creating Wang Laboratories in 1951. It's probably not an exaggeration to say that the United States would not be the technological powerhouse it is today without the contributions of Chinese and Chinese-Americans in its laboratories.

But at the same time, various estimates suggests that the China's government-orchestrated theft of trade secrets costs the United States tens of billions of dollars a year, if not hundreds of billions a year. And with those billions of dollars go many jobs that will never be created in the United States.

One other case that has hit the front pages in October 2018 is how the Chinese central bank and private sector entities connected to it targeted Equifax, the large credit reporting agency,[2] during the previous year. Hackers got away with driver's license and Social Security numbers of about 145 million Americans. But they were after more—they apparently wanted the secret algorithms that Equifax uses to rate individuals for their credit-worthiness. The Chinese have no equivalent because their financial system is so different. The central bank asked eight Chinese companies to help it build such a system, according to *The Wall Street Journal*. One of them was Ant Financial, a subsidiary of the enormous Alibaba Holding Group in Hangzhou.

The FBI investigated Daniel Zou, a Chinese-Canadian working in Toronto. He downloaded company documents and searched Equifax websites for the contact information of other ethnic Chinese employees. According to the *Journal*, the Ant unit of Alibaba offered to triple salaries for some of the Chinese Equifax employees and provided instructions on specific information they should bring with them. Zou denied any wrong-doing, but in January 2018, Chinese officials unveiled a state-backed credit reporting system and gave Ant Financial an 8 percent stake in the entity. And Zou now works for Ant Financial in Vancouver, Canada, a very happy and presumably prosperous man. Efforts to reach him for comment were unsuccessful.

Several other cases have been documented over a period of years affecting U.S. nuclear weapon technology, the blueprints for Boeing's C-17 cargo plane (which the U.S. military uses to move tanks and other heavy equipment around the world) and body designs for two different advanced jet fighters, the F-22 and the F-35, which is the latest jet fighter the Pentagon has developed and paid for. China's Huawei Technologies, the large telecommunications company, in 2003 admitted ripping off software that ran computer networking systems from Cisco Systems, the Silicon Valley networking giant. Micron Technology, a maker of DRAM semiconductor chips based in Boise, Idaho, in November 2018 prevailed in a California court over a Chinese state-owned company called Fujian Jinhua Integrated Circuit and Taiwan's United Microelectronics[3]. They were indicted for stealing Micron's intellectual property. If convicted, each company could face a fine of up to $20 billion. Note that a state-owned company was involved. That could have happened only if the leadership in Beijing authorized it or encouraged it.

The pattern reaches deeply into many sectors and geographies. "Chinese actors have stolen wind turbine technology in Wisconsin, agricultural research in Kansas, cancer drug research in Pennsylvania and software source code in New York," the criminal division of the U.S. Department of Justice said in a November 2018 statement[4].

Perhaps the most sensational case broke in October 2018 because it involved an official of China's MSS, Yanjun Xu, who sought to purloin jet engine technology from General Electric[5]. Military sources say the Chinese have made big strides in building jet fighters partly by borrowing technology from Russia and partly as a result of the stolen U.S. designs. But the quality of either Russian or Chinese engines does not yet match up with that of General Electric's. "This is not an isolated incident. It is part of an overall economic policy of developing China at America's expense," said John Demers, head of the Justice Department's national security division, in announcing Xu's arrest.[6] Note that it was the Justice Department, not the FBI, taking the lead, which is one possible clue that it has been rendered less effective because of the multi-year penetration operation. (Xu was also involved in seeking aerospace industry information from Ji Chaoqun, a United States Army reservist, as described in Chapter Six.)

Court papers identified Xu as a deputy division director of the Sixth Bureau of Jiangsu Province, a unit of the MSS. Prosecutors alleged that Xu worked from 2013 through 2018 with several Chinese universities to obtain proprietary information from U.S. aviation and aerospace companies. Part of his strategy was recruiting ethnic Chinese employees from those companies to travel to China for what he called an exchange of ideas. At GE Aviation, his target seemed to be information about composite materials the company used in making fan blades and other components of the engine. Fans are important components because of the tremendous heat generated in a jet engine.

According to the 16-page indictment[7], an unidentified and unindicted co-conspirator (Employee 1) approached an employee (Employee 2) at GE Aviation—no ethnicities were revealed, but they almost certainly spoke Mandarin Chinese— in March 2017 and invited Employee 2 on an all-expense-paid trip to China to meet with scientists at Nanjing University of Aeronautics and Astronautics, which is regarded as one of the top engineering universities in China. There, he was introduced to Xu, who was using an alias, Qu Hui, and disguising his true identity. Employee 2 gave a presentation at the university which contained some details of GE's engines. He received $3,500 for his presentation and as reimbursement for his expenses.

Xu remained in contact with Employee 2 via email and the following January, in 2018, invited him back to China and told him to bring information about GE Aviation's "system specifications, design process." Xu kept asking for more details about GE's fan blade design. Employee 2 at some point even sent Xu a file directory of documents on his company-issued laptop.

At some point, GE must have become aware of the pattern of contacts because the Justice Department and FBI were brought in. Employee 2, presumably cooperating by now with U.S officials, never went to China again but proposed that Xu travel to Brussels, Belgium, where Employee 2 would meet him and hand over a thumb drive containing the contents of

Employee 2's laptop. "The computer you bring along is the company computer, right?" Xu asked.

Xu was caught when he arrived in Brussels in a sting operation and extradited to the United States. He is the first and only Chinese intelligence official to be detained by American authorities. Officers of the PLA have been indicted, as have officials of Chinese state-owned enterprises, but they remained in China and hence were not subject to arrest.

The Xu case is extraordinary because it demonstrates that the Chinese government itself is directly involved in creating strategies to steal American secrets. GE Aviation said Xu was not successful in penetrating its operations in the Cincinnati area, where its headquarters is located. It is not known what happened to the two GE employees.

Think of the scale of what could be happening. MSS is an organization with 100,000 employees, with 40,000 of them based outside of China, according to Wikipedia.[8] Hundreds of PLA officers and experts also are said to be assigned to the ministry's headquarters. And provincial units of the MSS are engaged in international espionage and penetration operations as well, particularly the Jiangsu office. Let's postulate that 5,000 Chinese government officials and agents may be seeking American technology secrets at any given time.

One clear strategy is approaching Chinese who have been educated in American universities and gone to work at American companies or research institutions. The ancestors of most of the 4 million Chinese-Americans fled southern Guangdong and Fujian provinces and never spoke Mandarin Chinese and perhaps no longer speak their own dialects at all. Many fled the Communist takeover of China in 1949 or the disastrous Cultural Revolution (1966-76) and have little common cause with Beijing. The Chinese who were imported to build American railroads have long ago lost contact with family members remaining in China. The vast majority of the people we call Chinese-Americans (a vague phrase that encompasses a broad gamut of people and backgrounds) have embraced the American system.

But there are 350,000 Chinese students at American universities today, according to the Institute for International Education, and tens of thousands of others have graduated and are working at American companies or institutions on visas. An undetermined number of others, certainly thousands, have obtained U.S. citizenship, which does not necessarily mean that they have declared loyalty to the American democracy. It may be simply a device that allows them to continue their work. Most of these Chinese are focused on science, technology, engineering and math (STEM) fields, such as artificial intelligence, materials, nanoscience and robotics.

MSS and its affiliates can approach these thousands of former students and other Chinese individuals directly inside the United States. "They could be subject to contact and recruitment even in their social environment," Campbell, the former FBI official, told me. "We've seen it where these employees are approached at grocery stores and churches and social functions, and even their family members can be targeted as well."

Or MSS can work through the former students' families back in China, which is a double-edged sword. If a Chinese working at an American company declines to cooperate, the repercussions are obvious—the family back home will be made to suffer. "If they are aware of threats against and interrogations of their grandmothers in Chengdu, you almost can't blame Chinese people who are being put under immense pressure to turn over information to the Chinese government," Minky Worden, a senior official of

Human Rights Watch, who has spent 30 years studying China, told me. "The students grew up within the Communist system so they know that when the government threatens your relatives, they mean business. They have every reason to believe that Chinese government will fulfill threats that are used to extract information. What kind of government weaponizes its own students? Yet that's what the PRC (People's Republic of China) has been willing to do." On the other side of the coin, if the Chinese researcher working in the United States cooperates and succeeds in acquiring a desired technology, the family will benefit, either directly or indirectly.

If 5,000 agents have thousands of targets inside American companies and institutions, it is easily conceivable that there could be dozens of operations targeting technologies at any one given point in time, overwhelming U.S. governmental agencies. Further complicating matters, MSS and its affiliates may make the approach decades after a Chinese-born employee has joined a company and worked his or her way into a position of deep knowledge and trust. Zheng, who was arrested in the GE turbine case in upstate New York, was 55 years of age and had been working for the company for 10 years. He may have worked loyally for GE for a number of years before even being tempted to start stealing secrets.

This is another case of the Chinese party-state being able to exploit their population's sheer numbers over a long period of time. "They send individuals as students around the world," former FBI official Campbell told me. "From some of them, they eventually request some sort of payback for the ability to be educated in these other geographies. They are able to seed these individuals as potential intelligence collectors and purveyors of information to help them grow their industries. It really shows this concerted holistic whole-of-government effort by the Chinese government focusing on the technological area. It's really starting to reap benefits for them as we are seeing with the cases that are being prosecuted by the Justice Department."

Could U.S. companies monitor the activities of all ethnic Chinese employees? This gets into very sensitive racial and legal realms. Equifax executives discussed monitoring all its Chinese employees but then concluded it was against American law. Moreover, some Chinese employees and government officials have been unfairly accused and the charges against them dropped. Asian-American politicians complain that ethnic Chinese employees are targeted for surveillance far more often than are employees of other ethnicities.

It is true that American investigators appear to have made mistakes in targeting a number of Chinese-Americans believed to have betrayed secrets. The HuffPost ran a story in April 2018 by Kimberly Yam about an espionage case against Sherry Chen, a hydrologist with the National Weather Service, which is part of the Department of Commerce.[i] FBI agents arrested Chen in 2014, accusing her of using a stolen password to obtain information about U.S. dams and lying about a meeting with a Chinese official. She lost her job. Yet a week before Chen was going to go on trial, the case was dropped with no explanation. Chen was able to appeal her termination with the U.S. Merit Systems Protection Board, an independent agency, and regain her job. "It's clear that Sherry Chen was the victim of gross injustice and unwarranted racial profiling during her time at the [Commerce] Department," Rep. Ted Lieu (D-Calif.) was quoted as saying.

The article continued: "Several Asian-American legislators applauded the decision and are now calling for an investigation into the handling of Chen's case. 'Unfortunately, there have been multiple cases in which Chinese-American scientists like Sherry have been wrongfully targeted and arrested for alleged espionage only to have those charges dropped with no explanation,' Rep. Judy Chu (D-Calif.) said in a statement. 'That is why (the Congressional Asian Pacific American Caucus) has made it a top priority to urge the Department of Justice to examine whether there is a pattern or practice of Asian Americans being singled out by federal law enforcement and prosecutors for espionage.'

"As the legislators pointed out, Chen is among a string of scientists and researchers of Asian descent who have been wrongly accused of espionage, including Chinese-American professor Xiaoxing Xi, Eli Lilly scientists Guoqing Cao and Shuyu Li, and NASA contract worker Bo Jiang.

"Research shows that Americans of Asian descent are disproportionately profiled in espionage cases. The nonpartisan Chinese-American organization, Committee of 100, published a white paper last June revealing Asians were more likely to be charged with economic espionage than people of any other race."

This is why the issue of what to do about China's economic spies is so difficult. China's ability to conceal its actions depends in part on having a large community of Chinese-Americans who are perfectly innocent. Efforts to counter-attack the espionage run smack into charges of racial profiling and discrimination. The HuffPost article did not mention any of the documented cases in which Chinese living in the United States, whether citizens or not, have been caught stealing secrets, a revealing gap in Ms. Yam's reporting. It appears that some Chinese-Americans are attempting to create a smokescreen in which any enforcement effort is seen as racial profiling. The reason more Chinese and recent Chinese-Americans are targeted is because China, the world's second largest power, is engaged in a multipronged campaign to steal or acquire sensitive American technologies. The secrets keep flowing out.

* * *

The Micron case, mentioned briefly above, is noteworthy because it followed an entirely different pattern that involved Taiwanese nationals and further underscores how Chinese state-backed entities are engaged in ambitious schemes to build new industries on the basis of stolen IP.

Because China is the manufacturing platform for so many electronic products, it depends on the import of semiconductors or on the production of those semiconductors in China by American, South Korean or Taiwanese companies. The most basic semiconductors are DRAMS, which store memory and hence the name, Dynamic Random-Access Memory. China wants to break into the DRAM business and so in February 2016 two state-owned enterprises created Fujian Jinhua Integrated Circuit Co., known as Jinhua. It was created with an impressive $5.65 billion in funding from the Chinese government and related entities, according to court documents. It started building a factory in Fujian Province, directly across the Taiwan Straits from Taiwan.

The only problem was that it did not know how to make DRAMs.

Micron, meanwhile, made some DRAMs in a subsidiary in Taiwan, managed by Chen Zhengkun, also known as Stephen Chen. He must have been quietly negotiating with representatives from Jinhua over a period of time. He resigned from Micron in July 2015 and began working for a Taiwanese company called, United Microelectronics Corporation. Soon thereafter, United began talking with Jinhua about a technology cooperation agreement. Big money was at stake. Jinhua agreed to pay $300 million for the necessary equipment to make DRAMs and would pay an additional $400 million based on progress in DRAM development. Taiwan's government approved the deal. Chen's own personal compensation was also likely to increase substantially.

Chen next left United and made the jump to Jinhua, where he became president in charge of the DRAM production facility. He may have spent time at the Taiwanese company as a means of not drawing attention to a direct move from Micron to a Chinese entity.

He and two co-conspirators took with them massive amounts of information about how Micron makes DRAMs. One based in the United States stole 900 Micron files containing proprietary information, including data about future generations of DRAMs that were still in the research and development stage. He made the apparent mistake of storing the files on his Google Drive account located on servers in the United States. Investigators found them.

The complaint against the three Taiwanese by the United States District Court for the Northern District of California identified eight specific trade secrets that the Taiwanese stole. A grand jury indicted them.

The U.S. Department of Commerce barred Jinhua from buying American components, which was expected to cripple the company[9]. But being backed by the full faith and guarantee of the Chinese government, Jinhua will almost certainly keep trying to break into the semiconductor industry—through any means necessary.

* * *

Not all efforts by China's party-state to obtain secrets are as secretive or subtle. One case that broke in January 2019 was the equivalent of a flagrant foul in American basketball jargon. Huawei (pronounced hwa-way) Technologies, now the world's largest manufacturer of equipment that make up telecommunications networks, was indicted for brazenly attempting to steal technology from a T-Mobile laboratory in Bellevue, Wa., near Seattle. In a meticulously well-documented 28-page indictment filed in the United States District Court for the Western District of Washington at Seattle[10], prosecutors described how Huawei started selling cheaper smartphones to T-Mobile for sale in the United States. T-Mobile had spent a great deal of money and gone to great lengths to create a robot called Tappy that tested the phones it sold to see how well their hardware and software performed. It was nicknamed Tappy because of the way it tapped the phones' screens. This automated testing system obviously gave T-Mobile a competitive advantage in the market—its phones did not break or malfunction as often as others. T-Mobile recognized that Tappy was a competitive tool and allowed only scientists and engineers with special badges to enter a secure laboratory in Bellevue, complete with security cameras and human guards, where Tappy resided.

T-Mobile allowed a few employees from each company that supplied it with phones to enter the lab so that they could see for themselves what the testing results showed regarding the phones their companies had manufactured. Starting in 2012, T-Mobile extended that privilege to Huawei employees after the Chinese company signed non-disclosure agreements and promised not to take pictures of Tappy or attempt to reverse engineer it.

But Huawei wanted to make a perfect copy of Tappy and was working on its own version of a robotic testing system back in China. Its employees with special badges kept getting emails from China urging them to obtain more precise measurements and other technical details, which they tried to do. (The fact that so many Huawei employees used email to conduct an attack on a U.S. laboratory is what ultimately created an electronic trail.) The Huawei employees with access to the T-Mobile lab pleaded with their more senior colleagues to stop asking for so much information, which T-Mobile employees simply would not divulge. T-Mobile "is VERY angry the questions we asked (sic)," one email read. "Sorry we can't deliver any more information to you."

Ultimately, two Huawei employees were caught stealing technical information in May 2013. One of them, identified only as A.X., actually took a robotic arm from Tappy out of the lab, went home and photographed it. He then sent the details via email to his superiors in China. A.X. returned the robotic arm the next day, saying it was a "mistake" to have taken it home by accident. T-Mobile confronted Huawei, which launched its own internal investigation. It argued to T-Mobile that the two employees were rogue players acting on their own. T-Mobile did not buy it.

As all of this was unfolding in Washington state, and while Huawei was insisting that the actions of the two engineers were "isolated," Huawei launched a bonus program to reward employees who stole confidential information from competitors, the indictment alleged. "Employees were directed to post confidential information obtained from other companies on an internal Huawei website or, in the case of especially sensitive information, to send an encrypted email to a special email mailbox," it said. A so-called "competition management group" reviewed the submissions and awarded monthly bonuses to employees who provided the most valuable stolen information.

T-Mobile brought a civil suit against Huawei shortly thereafter. It's not clear why it took the U.S. Department of Justice so many years to bring a criminal case. But it would appear that as Huawei has emerged as the key Chinese company at the heart of U.S.-Chinese trade and technology frictions, federal authorities decided to make an example of the case to bring greater pressure to bear on Huawei.

3 Chinese Students and Their Systematic Recruitment

To walk across the campus of a major university, such as Columbia University in upper Manhattan, is to be immersed in the distinctive Mandarin Chinese language, as if you were walking down a street in Beijing. It would be irresponsible for me to approach these Chinese students directly because no matter what they might tell me, I would be putting them at risk. Other students might report on them for having contact with an American journalist. It's well-known that some of the students report on the activities of others. But no one seems to know precisely who is informing on whom.

What these students have gone through to arrive at American universities is impressive. They have paid for multiple years of extra English lessons beyond what they learned in school, according to Terry Crawford, chief executive of InitialView, a company that records videos with international students applying to American universities. He described the process in the *Chronicle of Higher Education* in May 2018.[1] Crawford obviously has a vested interest in seeing the practice continue, but his deep involvement also gives him insight.

The students also have to pay for tuition at schools that prepare them to apply abroad. "When they take the SAT or ACT, they usually have to fly to another country, and most students take those exams, as well as the TEOFL, several times," he explained. All that costs more money. "In addition, the students have potentially paid $10,000 for professional application advice from a college-advising agent. And all of this is for the privilege of applying to American institutions that charge them more—in some cases more than double—than what they charge domestic students."

The reason they go through the trouble and expense is that they believe an exposure to American universities and the scientific research that is taking place there will enhance their career prospects, whether it is in the United States or back home in China. They also have the wealth to afford it. Chinese students make up the largest bloc among all foreign students studying in the United States.

For years, as the trend has rapidly expanded, many Americans believed that these universities were exposing the Chinese students to freedom of expression and opinion, concepts that they would take home with them, perhaps challenging the rigid authoritarianism that China has embraced. "If we aren't careful, the United States will squander one of its strategic advantages: the good will it has with China's best and brightest," Crawford wrote.

But Crawford is naïve if he thinks that Chinese students are studying American political history and the ideals that shaped the nation. They are targeted primarily on technology sectors. There's certainly no evidence that going to an American university will somehow turn them into democracy advocates back home or that they can defend American interests if and when they go back home. The young Chinese students I have worked with in my role as president of the Overseas Press Club Foundation realize that the values of free speech and freedom of the press simply cannot be practiced if they go home. I've presented several scholarships to Chinese students enrolled in American universities who wish to become journalists, but then watched them struggle with the central reality—they can go home but they cannot openly espouse the values they have learned here.

Economically speaking, American universities have come to depend on the income from foreign students. Although the total numbers of foreign students at American universities declined in the 2017-2018 academic year, the Institute of International Education says foreign students pumped $42 billion into U.S. educational institutions in a single year[2]. Chinese money accounts for about a third of that. The universities are under pressure because of a decline in the number of U.S. high school students graduating each year and cutbacks in state funding in some cases.

Many university officials either are not aware of potential risks or pretend they do not exist. Philip J. Hanlon, president of Dartmouth College, and Matthew J. Slaughter, dean of its Tuck School of Business, argued that Chinese students are making a net positive impact on universities and on the American economy. "The outsize and growing role of Chinese students in American innovation is especially evident in science, technology, engineering and mathematics," they wrote in an op ed in the *Wall Street Journal* in November 2018.[3] "Chinese students in U.S. STEM programs are often more productive than students from other countries."

There's no question that Chinese students are contributing to research in American institutions. But the Dartmouth authors simply did not mention the fact that at least a portion of Chinese graduates of American universities working at American companies and institutes are a primary recruiting ground for the MSS or that the leaders of China's technology development efforts routinely recruit them.

At the opposite end of the spectrum from an academic point of view, it is not true that every Chinese student has espionage on his or her mind despite a remark to that effect from President Trump. At one point during a dinner at his New Jersey golf course, Trump noted of an unnamed country, clearly China, that "almost every student that comes over to this country is a spy," according to Politico.[4]

The truth lies somewhere in between. A student does not have to become an economic espionage agent to absorb very useful knowledge about AI or robotics or other sensitive fields. In fact, American universities are eager for Chinese students to work in some of the most cutting edge labs because of their knowledge and determination.

Michael Wessel, a commissioner of the congressional U.S.-China Economic and Security Review Commission, told the House Science, Space and Technology Committee in April 2018 about two labs where Chinese graduate students had a strong presence.[5] The first was the Berkeley Artificial Intelligence Research (BAIR) lab at the University of California at Berkeley. This is a leading facility working on advanced computer vision, machine learning, natural language processing and robotics. "Roughly 20 percent of the PhD students at BAIR are PRC nationals," he said. (PRC stands for the People's Republic of China.)

The second was at the University of Maryland's Bing Nano Research Group. It works on materials science, which has implications for energy storage and biomaterials. "Thirty of the 38 post-doctoral researchers and graduate students are from China," Wessel testified. "Every one of the visiting professors and professors utilizing 'J' visas are from China." This lab, he noted, is supported by the National Aerospace and Science Administration (NASA), the Pentagon's Defense Advanced Research Projects Agency (DARPA), the Air Force Office of Scientific Research and the Department of Energy.

Because it has gotten slightly more difficult for Chinese students to get work visas and remain in the United States under the Trump administration, students such as the ones at Berkeley and Maryland may simply decide to take their knowledge home.

Mancini, the cyberforensics expert at Seton Hill, is particularly critical of that pattern. "They are flooding us with students," Mancini told me. "And these students are doing top-rate research and development. The universities love it because they also are paying top dollar to attend.

"Maybe a few try to stay here. But others probably say to themselves. 'Okay, I've gone to school and it's time to go home. What am I taking back? I'm taking back years of research and development. I don't have to breach the university. I did the research with the professor and all the other smart kids. It's all on my thumb drive. I'm going back to the motherland. See ya later.' They are going to bring back the knowledge. I absolutely think it is a concerted effort."

There's no indication that the Chinese government identifies specific students and instructs them to go to specific American universities to obtain particular technological insights. But after individual students and their families have made the commitment to send a child to an American university, leaders of different technology efforts in China do consciously target these students and recent graduates for recruitment to jobs back home. "The motherland needs you. The motherland welcomes you. The motherland places her hope in you." Those messages, in Chinese characters only, are at the top of both the English and Chinese versions of the website of China's "Thousand Talent Plan." (www.1000plan.org) For that insight, I am indebted to Yangyang Cheng, writing in ChinaFile.[6]

The Thousand Talent Plan has drawn the FBI's attention. "The Chinese government is already far ahead of us in creating direct financial incentives for gifted scientists and researchers to relocate and do work in their country," E.W.

Priestap, assistant director of the FBI's Counterintelligence Division told the Senate Judiciary Committee[7]. "The Chinese government has created comprehensive programs to identify, develop, and retain their most talented citizens. These talent recruitment and 'brain gain' programs (as some in China call them) also encourage theft of intellectual property from U.S. institutions. For example, China's talent recruitment plans, such as the Thousand Talents Program, offer competitive salaries, state-of-the-art research facilities, and honorific titles, luring both Chinese overseas talent and foreign experts alike to bring their knowledge and experience to China, even if that means stealing proprietary information or violating export controls to do so."

Being recruited to go home does not necessarily mean that a Chinese scientist is stealing proprietary information. It could be that the scientist participated in the creation of that knowledge. In June 2018, Li Yuan, then a reporter for *The Wall Street Journal*, provided an insight into how the recruitment process works[8]. Li described how Ye Tianchun, who heads China's research into semiconductors, went to Santa Clara, Ca., in Silicon Valley near the headquarters of American chip giant Intel. It was obviously a highly symbolic location—on the doorstep of America's biggest chip company. More than 300 people, the majority of them Chinese and Chinese-Americans, packed a convention center hall to hear about job opportunities in China. Ye spoke in Mandarin so if it were not for a Chinese-speaker working for the *Journal*, the event would have escaped broader American attention.

Luring employees across national borders is entirely legal and well within international norms. But it is nonetheless a powerful channel for attracting talent.

Reporter Li described how Alibaba and search engine giant Baidu have research-and-development offices in Silicon

Valley. A three-story building called Z-Park, was established by a Beijing government company to serve as a hub for Chinese tech companies and venture capital funds. In short, it is a systematic, organized effort backed by the city of Beijing's government, which means it has the party-state's backing.

Li described the story of one young Chinese woman, Gu Junli, who completed a doctorate in computer engineering at a prestigious university in China and then headed to Silicon Valley. Hers is a slight variation on the theme, but nonetheless illustrates how expertise can move. She interned at Google's headquarters, then joined chip maker Advanced Micro Devices, where she worked on big data and artificial intelligence, before going to Tesla as the lead expert for the electric-vehicle maker's autopilot unit.

Less than two years later, Gu jumped again to Xiaopeng Motors, a Chinese electric vehicles startup supported by tech giant Alibaba. She did not have to purloin any files. The knowledge was in her head.

Professors and other experts argue that it is the very openness of the American academic R&D scene that makes it so vibrant. But security officials see it through a different lens, warning about a new kind of intelligence collector. "The use of nontraditional collectors, especially in the academic setting, whether it's professors, scientists or students, we see in almost every field office that the FBI has around the country," FBI Director Wray testified before the Senate Intelligence Committee in February 2018[9]. "It's not just in major cities. It's in small ones as well. It's basically across every discipline.

"I think the level of naïveté on the part of the academic sector about this creates its own issues," Wray added. "They (China's party-state) are exploiting the very open research and development environment that we have, which we all revere, but they're taking advantage of it."

* * *

One case that illustrates how Chinese researchers have exploited the American research system was that of the National Institutes of Health, which is one of the most important funders of advanced medical research in the United States. The institutes receive federal funding, meaning taxpayer dollars, to then distribute to medical researchers in the form of research grants. They study cancer, heart disease, diabetes and many other conditions. The institutes, which have an enormous budget of $39 billion in 2019, operate on the basis of trust among researchers. Every grant request is subjected to a system of peer review, meaning fellow researchers are tapped to evaluate the scientific merit of what a peer is proposing to research. Information in the grant requests is supposed to be confidential and the assumption is that the winner of an NIH grant will perform the research at one of the roughly 10,000 NIH grant American institutions without any other governments involved.

But in the summer of 2018, NIH director Francis Collins told Congress that NIH was investigating about six research institutions on suspicions that researchers had failed to disclose financial contributions from other governments. "We are concerned about circumstances where people have intentionally been deceptive about those connections, with an intention to divert intellectual property or perhaps use their access to peer-review materials to ship them overseas," Collins told reporters after the congressional hearing.[10] China was obviously the greatest cause of concern.

Collins wrote to all grant institutions and asked them to set up briefings with FBI field offices to learn how to better protect their research. He also commissioned a report by M.

Roy Wilson, the co-chair of the NIH's advisory committee and the president of Wayne State University in Detroit. It turned out the problem was far greater than initially recognized. Wilson concluded that Chinese and Chinese-American researchers—whether graduate students or professors—were taking ideas from the supposedly confidential peer-review materials and either trying to develop those ideas at "shadow laboratories" in China or handing the information to different arms of the Chinese government. Some were taking ideas and applying for Chinese government funding as part of the Thousand Talents Program. In short, they were seeking to develop the technology and commercialize it before American researchers could. It was a pattern. "It's not just random here or there," Wilson said. "It is significant."[11]

This is not, strictly speaking, economic espionage where an individual steals secrets from a company, but the net effect is the same. "Unfortunately, some foreign governments have initiated systematic programs to unduly influence and capitalize on U.S.-conducted research," Wilson's panel concluded. Again, it was clear that the main focus was China's government.

This obviously represents a threat to the open research environment that American scientists are passionate about. "NIH has basically been operating on the principle that everyone is well-intentioned," Scott Kennedy, an expert on Chinese economic policy at the Center for Strategic and International Studies (CSIS) in Washington, D.C., told *The New York Times*.[12] "Then they run smack dab into the challenge of China, which has millions of researchers scrambling for money and for fame and for national glory. That creates an environment where some people may feel pressure to skirt, ignore or break the rules."

4 Buying Distressed or Undervalued U.S. Companies

When I first met David Vieau in researching my 2011 book, *The Next American Economy*[1], I thought he was leading a fascinating experiment in how America could carve out a position in one of the technologies of the future, in this case, lithium-ion batteries. Vieau (pronounced 'view') was chief executive officer of A123 Systems in a suburb of Boston. Lithium-ion batteries were then, and are still today, essential in building all-electric or hybrid vehicles and also important in storing wind and solar energy. Those sources of energy are highly variable depending on weather conditions so their power must be stored in batteries until humans need it. The key technology for A123's batteries came out of the Massachusetts Institute of Technology (MIT) in nearby Cambridge.

President Barack Obama and his team were big believers in A123. When they took office in early 2009, the American auto industry was in deep crisis and oil prices were an exorbitant $150 a barrel. "Obama's advance people came to me and asked, 'What do you need to accelerate the adoption of electric vehicles?" Vieau recalls.

A123 was selling batteries to Black & Decker for its power tools, so it had real customers. But it needed automotive customers and also more capital to work with. Obama personally told Vieau that his government would create customers for it. "We'll tee up the demand," Vieau recalls Obama telling him in a meeting. "You deliver on the demand."

His Department of Energy granted a $500 million loan to Fisker Automotive in Delaware and another $500 million loan to Tesla Motors in California. Both would be customers. And it gave A123 a $249 million matching grant to spend on building factories, not on operating expenses. At about the same time, the energy department probably made a mistake in supporting a California solar thin-film cell start-up called Solyndra that did not yet have any customers.

The State of Michigan gave A123 another $23 million in incentives to build a factory in Michigan. Major companies such as General Electric, Motorola, and Qualcomm lent some form of support, whether as customers or board members. All this appeared to be a model of how the American system functions best—technologists in a university came up with an idea and licensed it to a start-up firm, major companies were interested and helpful, private sector investors were enthusiastic, and both a state and national government supported it.

Today, A123's factory in Michigan is pumping out hundreds of millions of dollars worth of lithium-ion battery systems a year. But A123 does not own the factory. The company went bankrupt. And its automotive-sector assets were acquired by China's Wanxiang Group Corp., the country's largest auto parts maker[2]. Wanxiang also was able to purchase Fisker, which also went bankrupt after the Obama administration made an abrupt shift in its policies in the face of a congressional Tea Party investigation into the government's support of Solyndra. "We had university, business and government cooperating to make this company happen—it was a tsunami of good events," Vieau told me, "but it was followed by a tsunami of bad events. The fundamentals of A123's businesses are operating very well today. It just couldn't withstand the turbulence of getting the electric car off the ground."

Instead of being a model for how the United States can carve out positions in critical technology, the A123 story became a debacle in which a Chinese company was able to buy U.S. technology assets for pennies on the dollar. It paid $257 million for the company after Vieau had raised $1 billion from private investors and spent $100 million in federal government money.

There were several strands of the A123 disaster. Obama was trying to push through his Affordable Care Act and Republicans told Vieau that if Obama insisted on enacting health care, they would drop support for Obama's energy sector proposals, a threat they made good on. Big Three automakers would not support the effort, at least not on a timely basis, and the oil industry also quietly fought against it because it might have created an alternative to their product and driven down oil prices.

The hearings on Solyndra forced Department of Energy officials to appear before a House committee to testify under hostile questioning. Under that kind of political pressure, they dropped support of their grants to Fisker, which cut back on its purchases of A123 batteries. Major auto companies such as BMW also encountered problems and delays in integrating lithium-ion batteries into their vehicles. The new electric vehicle customers that Obama had promised to create started disappearing. "Our investors could no longer stomach any continued investment of money in a company that didn't have active customers that were building products," recalls Vieau, who is now retired in Newport, R.I. "As the customers kept dropping, the investors backed out." That's what forced the company into bankruptcy. A123 offices in Michigan did not respond to requests for comment. Tesla was able to survive.

This was a case in which we are our own worst enemy. We stage political fights over developing new technologies and cannot find a consistent path to allow them to mature. Because of Wall Street's demands for strong quarterly earnings, few American companies are interested in buying a damaged asset even if it owns a promising technology. But the Chinese party-state and its companies and enterprises place value on these assets because they recognize that technology has a strategic value, not just financial value. It's not the fault of Wanxiang that they acquired A123 and Fisker. They were smart. The failure was that of the American system.

The Chinese government is clearly using acquisitions as part of its Made in China 2025 policy. For many years, there were virtually no Chinese acquisitions of American companies or divisions. Lenovo's purchase of IBM's personal computer division in 2005 stood alone. But under President Xi, Chinese investments soared for a period of time and shifted from being new greenfield manufacturing facilities to being acquisitions of existing corporate assets.

The March 2018 report by the United States Trade Representative's Office (USTR) speaks volumes[3]. To get an idea of the scale of Chinese acquisitions, USTR turned to the American Enterprise Institute (AEI), a conservative think tank in Washington, and to the Rhodium group, a research-based hedge fund in New York.

The two organizations collected data in slightly different ways but they show a clear pattern. AEI data show a 2,460 percent increase, with investment rising from $2.2 billion in 2011 to $53.7 billion in 2016. In 2017, Chinese investment in the United States totaled $24.2 billion, representing a significant year-on-year decline, but still marking the second-highest annual total on record. Likewise, Rhodium data shows cumulative Chinese investment into the

United States growing from a mere $4.9 billion in 2011 to $45.2 billion in 2016 – an increase of 843 percent.

It's the pattern of acquisitions that is so revealing. They were targeted in technologies that China is targeting in its various five-year plans and its Made in China 2025 plan. Consider just one field, aviation, where the Chinese want to build their own aviation industry so they no longer have to buy jetliners from Boeing and Airbus. The Aviation Industry Corporation of China (AVIC) is the key state-owned enterprise leading the effort and it has a variety of subsidiaries that are also involved. Here's seven acquisitions listed by the U.S. trade representative's report:

1 Epic Aircraft—acquired by China Aviation Industry General Aircraft Co. (CAIGA), an AVIC subsidiary, for $4.3 million in April 2010 after a bankruptcy judge approved the deal. The acquisition included Epic intellectual property and technology.

2 Teledyne Technologies (Continental Motors and Mattituck Services)—acquired by Technify Motors USA Inc., a subsidiary of AVIC International Holding Corporation, in December 2010 for $186 million. Continental Motors was a pioneer in the area of full authority digital engine control technology.

3 Cirrus Aircraft—acquired by CAIGA in February 2011 for $210 million. At the time of purchase, Cirrus was the second largest manufacturer of GA aircraft and the largest manufacturer of piston-engine powered GA aircraft.

4   Southern Avionics & Communications Inc.—acquired by Continental Motors Group in November 2014. Southern Avionics was a leader in avionics sales, installation, and service. The company represented most major global avionics manufacturers through distribution or representative agreements.

5   United Turbine and UT Aeroparts—acquired by Continental Motors Group in January 2015. United Turbine and UT Aeroparts provided turbine aircraft engine and accessory services.

6   Align Aerospace—acquired by AVIC International in April 2015. Align provided supply chain services for the aerospace industry and distributes fasteners and other hardware for aerospace original equipment manufacturers.

7   Danbury Aerospace—acquired by Continental Motors Group in April 2015. Danbury Aerospace specialized in engine design and certification. In October 2016, Danbury operations in San Antonio were closed, resulting in layoffs of 57 people.

Consider the range of technologies that were acquired—engine control technology, piston engine-powered aircraft, avionics (which are the high-value added piece of the business accounting for many command and control functions), turbine aircraft engines, supply chain services and engine design.

Clearly, those technologies, taken as a whole, would lend an enormous boost to China's efforts to develop its own aerospace industry, which in turn would threaten Boeing and its employees in the United States. With $3 trillion in foreign exchange reserves, the party-state could purchase Boeing outright but such an acquisition effort would trigger alarm bells in the United States because Boeing is a defense contractor and also a symbol of American economic prowess. The Japanese discovered that high-profile acquisitions trigger backlashes. Learning from that experience, the Chinese government's strategy has been to make under-the-radar purchases to avoid unwanted attention. And they use a variety of corporate vehicles to further disguise their patterns of acquisition.

The Chinese government has done much the same in industry after industry. USTR identified the same pattern in these fields: integrated circuits, information technology and electronics, biotechnology, industrial machinery and robotics, renewable energy and automotive.

The USTR report says the government arranges for state-owned banks to lend money to the Chinese acquirers of these assets. Chinese entrepreneurs who have made big splashes with multi-billion dollar acquisitions, such as HNA and Dalian Wanda, have had to quickly sell all or part of their purchases because they do not fall within the government's specified priorities. In short, the acquisition of smaller, often financially challenged American companies is part of the central government's technology vision.

The prose is not particularly graceful but this key conclusion from the report is powerful: "USTR determines that the Chinese government directs and unfairly facilitates the systematic investment in, and acquisition of, U.S. companies and assets by Chinese companies, to obtain cutting-edge technologies and intellectual property (IP) and generate large-scale technology transfer in industries deemed important by state industrial plans. The role of the state in directing and supporting this outbound investment strategy is pervasive, and evident at multiple levels of government – central, regional, and local. The government has devoted massive amounts of financing to encourage and facilitate outbound investment in areas it deems strategic. In support of this goal, China has enlisted a broad range of actors to support this effort, including SOEs (state-owned enterprises), state-backed funds, government policy banks, and private companies."

5 Venture Capital as a Point of Entry

One of the strengths of the Chinese government's campaign to secure American technologies is that it constantly shifts. If cyber attacks draw too much political attention, the Chinese government can ease back for a period of time only to resume at a later date in a slightly different form. If hacking is not working against a particular target, it can try to recruit an insider for purposes of espionage.

It was in the rough 2016 time frame that the U.S. Trade Representative's Office and the Committee on Foreign Investment in the United States (CFIUS), an interagency body managed by the Treasury Department, started zeroing in on China's pattern of acquisition of smaller companies in targeted industries, as described in the previous chapter. The Chinese must have realized that because Chinese direct investment in the U.S. fell to $29.4 billion in 2017, according to the 2018 Report to Congress by the U.S.-China Economic and Security Review Commission, a bipartisan group.[1]

It added: "Chinese venture capital investments in the United States have accelerated, however, with China representing the largest single foreign VC investor ($24 billion) in the United States cumulatively between 2016 and 2017, according to a recent U.S. government study."

So the pattern shifted—activity by China's venture capital industry exploded while traditional acquisitions declined. The Japanese, with the sole exception of Masayoshi Son's SoftBank, were never able to imitate the American venture capital system, but the Chinese have embraced it with great vigor and given it a unique twist—central, provincial and municipal governments lend money to Chinese VC funds to invest. Some state-owned enterprises also provide funding and at least one major state-backed university, Tsinghua, has a VC fund. American VCs raise their money from private investors and have no connection to government funding mechanisms.

The Chinese VC funds are particularly active in Silicon Valley and as a whole are now investing more money than American VC funds are.[2] All of which has rattled the Pentagon, which in the 2015-2016 time frame started a high-level discussion of what the next big defense technology would be. Defense Secretary Ashton Carter and the Joint Chiefs of Staff were discussing what "the third offset" would be. In military jargon, an offset is an advanced technological capability that gives American forces "overmatch," meaning they have clear superiority on the battlefield. During the Cold War against the Soviet Union, it was nuclear weapons and President Reagan's Strategic Defense Initiative that provided superiority. In the Gulf War, it was precision-guided missiles and stealth capabilities.

The defense planners recognized that many dual use technologies were evolving rapidly in the private sector—AI, machine learning, autonomous vehicles, robotics and drones. They wanted to learn who else in the world might be interested, particularly the Chinese government because of the sheer amount of capital it possesses.

The top brass turned to Raj Shah, head of what was called the Defense Innovation Unit Experimental, in Silicon Valley to come up with answers. This office is the Pentagon's effort to obtain a window into new technologies emerging in Silicon Valley that could have military uses. The office also tries to streamline the process of doing business with the Pentagon, which can be too difficult and too expensive for smaller companies in particular. It has smaller offices in other technology hot spots—Austin, Tex. and Boston—as well as Washington, D.C.

Shah turned to Michael A. Brown, the former CEO of Symantec, the largest of the cybersecurity companies that have sprung up in recent years, Brown, who lives in the Silicon Valley area, was a Presidential Innovation Fellow after leaving Symantec. The Pentagon declined to make Brown available for an interview, but a Silicon Valley source who followed Brown's work described it to me.

Brown and fellow researchers started research for a report. They identified an incredible 500 China-based investors in Silicon Valley and elsewhere. The investment vehicles took a number of different forms—angel investors, venture capitalists and private equity funds. They had names such as Westlake Capital (owned by the city of Hangzhou). "No one was doing the diligence of asking, 'Which municipal government is funding this?'" my source explained.

The Chinese VCs fit in particularly well to Californian culture because of the large number of Asian-Americans living there and a strong international presence in the Silicon Valley work force. Plus, the Californians like to brag that they are the fifth largest economy in the world[ii], having surpassed Britain, and there is a distinct chill in the air between California and old institutions based across the continent in Washington, D.C.

In that climate, entrepreneurs certainly were not asking where the Chinese venture capital money came from. "For the most part, if you spend time with entrepreneurs here, they are not worried about geopolitics," the source said. "They are not worried about who is providing the money. They are intensely focused on. 'How do I get the next dollar to keep my company going?'

The general view among entrepreneurs was that the Chinese venture capital funds were in some ways better than American VC funds because they were not as concerned with valuations, meaning the financial markets' market capitalization. Chinese venture capitalists also were not as concerned with getting large percentages of a company's shares and were not as focused on return on investment, known in the trade as ROI. "Money was not their primary concern," the source said. "Their primary concern was, 'How do we get a seat at the table and see what's happening in the innovation landscape?'"

It was as if at least some entrepreneurs were on a sugar high. "The entrepreneurs were saying, 'This is great. I'm getting several million dollars. My valuation is high and I'm not diluting my ownership stake. For me, it's win, win, win,'" the source explained. "The entrepreneurial culture is all about hustling. They were not going to focus on broader geopolitical issues."

But downsides emerged. One question was, what could the Chinese VC's learn about an entrepreneur's secret sauce? Plenty, it turned out. "From a technical perspective in the emerging technology areas, the Chinese investors and the technocratic class are pretty savvy," the source said. "From the training of their engineers to the massive amount of focus the government is putting on training students in STEM fields, understanding the technology is not the issue. When they get a seat at the table, as part of any venture capital process, with pitch decks and pitch sessions, they get a pretty detailed view of what you are trying to accomplish and what kind of personnel you have on your team as a startup. It's not very hard to get through to the magic sauce."

No American official knows whether the Chinese VCs that receive government funding have a reporting mechanism back to those governments, many of which are involved in shaping China's own technology strategy. It only stands to reason that governments expect something in return for their money. The Chinese VCs would not have to secure control of an emerging technology—they could learn enough about it to help shape an investment decision back in China. Simply reviewing a start-up's business plan, even without investing in the company, provides a signal about how a particular technology is developing. Knowing which way American technologists are headed in a particular field is valuable intelligence.

Brown discovered traces of other troubling patterns. Once the Chinese VC funds had identified valuable intellectual property and knew where it resided, he began to wonder if they were turning to the Ministry of State Security or other cyber hackers to go after it. The network security of most start-ups was virtually non-existent.

And why were new Chinese employees coming into some of the companies that were of interest to the VC funds? "Mike learned from the FBI that there was is a pretty strong profile of a middle-aged Chinese engineer getting hired who then stole IP," the source explained. "They had those conversations because Mike had several cases where CEOs of startups would say, 'Hey, can you connect me with the FBI? We hired a Chinese engineer and saw him uploading massive amounts of data to a Chinese company's server. This was out of his domain. It wasn't even part of his work.'"

You would expect a technology CEO living in Silicon Valley to be in favor of all flows of capital into American start-ups, but Brown instead grew increasingly worried. His report, which appeared in January 2018, was entitled, "China's Technology Transfer Strategy: How Chinese Investments in Emerging Technology Enable A Strategic Competitor to

Access the Crown Jewels of U.S. Innovation.[4]" It found that Chinese participation in venture-backed startups reached a record level of between 10 and 16 percent of all venture capital deals in the 2015-2017 time frame.

Brown recognized that the Chinese investors were particularly active in four fields: AI, robotics, Augmented Reality/Virtual Reality and financial technology. These are considered dual use technologies because they have uses in the civilian world and also increasingly in the military world. "The line demarcating products designed and used for commercial versus military purposes is blurring with these emerging technologies," Brown wrote.

Virtual Reality, for example, is used in gaming but is also used in simulators in the military, teaching pilots how to operate a particular aircraft, say. The same technologies used to identify criminals such as facial recognition software and image detection also are essential in the wars of the future that Pentagon planners are contemplating. Drones, robots and autonomous vehicles also figure prominently in those scenarios. These technologies are considered "foundational," meaning they will set the stage for entire new industries, much the same way that semiconductors set the stage for the entire computing revolution.

Historically, the U.S. military has had a window of opportunity to explore new technologies emerging in America before potential geopolitical rivals gain access to those technologies. It could impose export controls to prevent foreign powers from acquiring sensitive products and give itself time to understand how it might use a technology. The Pentagon has long assumed that it had a time advantage over potential adversaries.

But now, Chinese investors are obtaining insights into at least some new technologies before the Pentagon is aware of them. The Chinese VCs do not need to worry about export controls because they are taking away ideas, not finished products. All of which might give the Chinese a technological edge that could, conceivably, be converted into a military edge. "The U.S. does not have a comprehensive policy or the tools to address this massive technology transfer to China," the report concluded. "The U.S. government does not have a holistic view of how fast this technology transfer is occurring, the level of Chinese investment in U.S. technology, or what technologies we should be protecting."

Brown followed up with testimony before the House Permanent Select Committee on Intelligence in July, offering layer upon layer of details about what the Chinese venture capitalists were doing[5]. He said that because of the way the deal flow works in Silicon Valley, many different investors might see a company's pitch even if they do not choose to invest. "As a result, it's likely that Chinese investors, in aggregate, have seen upwards of half of recent U.S. venture financings," Brown told the committee. "Chinese investors have a broad view of U.S. innovation across a range of technologies. It's both logical and probable that China uses this as a vantage point from which to target specific technologies, including the underlying intellectual property (IP) and know how, as well (as to learn) about the key talent that best understand the technology."

The only government entity in a position to monitor Silicon Valley's outpouring of technology to the Chinese is the Committee on Foreign Investment (CFIUS), but it is still understaffed and underfunded, even after passage of the Foreign Investment Risk Review Modernization Act (FIRRMA) that took effect in the summer of 2018. CFIUS, which consists of representatives or observers from about 20 different U.S. agencies and bodies, now has the power to review investments by VCs even if they do not give the VC a controlling interest. But obtaining the expertise to adequately analyze those transactions in a timely manner is still in doubt.

Brown became head of the DIUX, which was renamed simply the Defense Innovation Unit, signifying that it was now a permanent body.

* * *

Some of the Chinese investment funds are affiliated with major Chinese technology companies, which have the nickname "BAT" for Baidu, Alibaba and Ten Cent. These are considered strategic investors and they have been able to take minority stakes in high-value technology companies without triggering any federal review. These companies are cash-rich so they do not need funding from any Chinese governmental unit, but they are nonetheless part of the party-state apparatus because they have been obliged to accept Communist Party cells inside their companies.

Baidu, for example, has invested about $75 million in Velodyne LiDAR, based in Morgan Hill, Ca. Velodyne makes the specialized lasers, called LiDARs, which stands for "light detection and ranging." These devices bounce beams of electrons off all objects within several hundred yards of a moving car and create a mental image in the car's control systems of where it is and what objects it might encounter. This is one of the technologies where Chinese automakers are competing neck-to-neck with American industry. Velodyne has been smart enough not to give away its crown jewels, but Baidu is bound to obtain some insights as a result of its investment.

Is it reciprocal? Again, that's the burning question. American VC's also are active in China, but they are trying to simply make money. They are transaction-oriented. They have little interest in controlling underlying technologies and there are no reports of Americans obtaining access to Chinese technology through their investments, much less funneling that information back to a government agency seeking to benefit from the knowledge. There is a strategic dimension to what Chinese VC funds are doing in the United States that is lacking in what American funds are doing in China.

Now that CFIUS has been strengthened and Brown has made such an impact, McKinsey & Co., the consultancy, expects Chinese VC investments in Silicon Valley will decline in 2019. "No Chinese company wants to be caught up for months in a review process with the Committee on Foreign Investment in the United States (CFIUS), with the high risk of the transaction being turned down," the consultancy said.[6] "As a result, many Chinese strategic investors are simply self-censoring and not taking opportunities to make acquisitions in the United States, or they are turning to smaller amounts of organic investment."

But the Chinese won't simply disappear. The game will merely shift. Two other patterns of technology acquisition have emerged. In the first, Chinese government-related interests acquire or set up a company that does not appear to be Chinese in origin. It then seeks to buy sensitive U.S. technology and export it from the United States. It happened with a company called Global IP, founded by Emil Youssefzadeh and Umar Javed and based in Los Angeles. Global IP told Boeing it wanted to buy a satellite to provide better Internet access for Africa.[7] Boeing started making the satellite.

In reality, the largest investor in the company was China Orient Asset Management Co., which funneled financing through offshore firms in the British Virgin Islands. But there was a falling out between the two founders and their Chinese backers and they quit. They blew the whistle that the company had been taken over by Chinese interests, who presumably would have diverted the satellite to the Chinese military, which could have repurposed it. Boeing cancelled the deal. There could be many more deals such as this one that completely escape attention. This one came to light only because of the dispute between Youssefzadeh and Javed and their Chinese backers.

A second pattern is that a Chinese company with an R&D lab in the United States comes up with a product that is more advanced than what the company could create in China and seeks to export the product, in effect, back to itself, meaning to China. Huawei—though effectively blocked from selling its telecom gear in the United States—has a research and development center in Santa Clara, Calif., the heart of Silicon Valley.[8] It is run by the company's R&D arm, FutureWei Technologies Inc. It employees 700 engineers and scientists, presumably a mix of many nationalities and skill sets. The U.S. Commerce Department has issued export licenses in the past to allow FutureWei to send technology back to Huawei in China, but in January 2019 it decided against granting a license for the export of software that included high-speed data-transfer technology. How many other Chinese entities are exporting technology back to China, with or without U.S. government approval, and what are they exporting? No one on the American side of the equation knows the full story.

PART TWO

Shaping American Opinion
and Decision-Making

"Draw opponents in with
the prospect of gain.
Take them by confusion."

—Sun Tzu

6 Penetrating Governmental Institutions

It was one of the most astonishing penetrations of the FBI by a foreign agent in recent history. Kun Shan Chun, known as Joey Chun, was a Chinese national who became a naturalized U.S. citizen. He began working at the FBI's New York Field Office in 1997 as an electronics technician assigned to the Computerized Central Monitoring Facility of the FBI's Technical Branch. He worked out so well that the next year, in 1998, the agency gave him a Top Secret security clearance. He had access to classified information.[1]

The FBI, in reconstructing his tale of betrayal, believes Chun started out in 2005 by funneling technical information to a company that his relatives established in China called Zhuhai Kolion Technology Company. Chun had an indirect financial interest in the company, including through an investment made by one of his relatives. Other Chinese nationals—they are not identified—asked Chun to conduct research and consulting in the United States, supposedly to support Kolion, and Chun obliged them. He received partial compensation for international trips as well as cash payments to a relative.

Chun was introduced to someone identified in court records as "Chinese official-1" in 2007 and started providing him with information. On a trip that Chun made to Italy and France, the Chinese official clearly identified himself although he was not identified in court papers. Chun knew exactly what he was doing. He continued to meet the official on different international trips.

The list of types of information that he provided could have allowed the MSS to render the FBI largely ineffective in at least some situations. Chun disclosed information regarding the FBI's personnel, structure, and technological capabilities, including general information regarding the FBI's surveillance strategies and certain categories of surveillance targets.

In 2012, the FBI started a routine investigation of Chun's Top Secret security clearance. But Chun repeatedly lied on standardized forms about his contacts with foreign nationals. Chun reported that he traveled to Hong Kong and China nine times, as well as to Canada, Thailand, Europe, Australia and New Zealand. It's not known how many of those trips involved meeting the Chinese official.

The damage that Chun inflicted continued to mount. In 2013, Chun downloaded an FBI organizational chart from his FBI computer in Manhattan. He edited the chart to remove the names of FBI personnel and then saved the document on a piece of digital media that he sent to the Chinese official.

The Chinese official kept asking for more. In January 2015, he asked Chun for information regarding technology used by the FBI. Chun took pictures of documents displayed in a restricted area of the FBI's New York Field Office, which contained details of multiple surveillance technologies that the agency used. Chun sent the photos to his personal cell phone and later transmitted them.

The FBI grew increasingly suspicious and arranged for an undercover FBI employee to meet Chun. The undercover employee posed as an independent contractor. He must have spoken Chinese.

In recorded conversations, Chun revealed his relationship with the Kolion company and Chinese nationals. He boasted that Kolion had government backing and said he had met someone he believed to be a section chief in the Chinese government.

In June 2015, Chun told the undercover agent that he had mentioned him to his Chinese contacts and they were interested in what the undercover agent had, presumably technical details of some sort. As the meetings continued, Chun said he knew that the Chinese government was recruiting individuals who could provide help and that they were willing to provide immigration benefits and other compensation in exchange. Chun wanted a cut of the action as a "subconsultant."

The FBI arrested him on March 16, 2016 and he subsequently confessed to his crimes. He was sentenced to 24 months in federal prison. "This investigation validates that we at the FBI are not immune to the threat of an insider," said FBI Assistant Director-in-Charge William F. Sweeney Jr.[2] That can only be considered a classic understatement. The net effect of what Chun revealed over more than a decade would have allowed the MSS to create a comprehensive view of how the FBI operated, the technologies it used, who it surveilled and how it surveilled them. The complete damage that Chun inflicted will almost certainly never be revealed.

* * *

The FBI was able to break up at least one other effort to penetrate an American institution, this time, the U.S. Army.[3] In September 2018, the FBI arrested Ji Chaoqun, 27, for providing information about employees of American defense contractors to Chinese intelligence officers and lying about his contacts with those officers while applying for a U.S. Army program that grants accelerated citizenship rights to enlistees. Among the factors that tripped him up: his Apple iCloud text message database preserved many incriminating details.

Ji was apparently recognized as a potential intelligence asset before he left China to attend the Illinois Institute of Technology in Chicago. He spent two years there and received a master's degree in electrical engineering in 2015.

During that time, he was in touch with the Jiangsu Province branch of the MSS and Xu, the MSS official who was later arrested in Belgium and extradited to the United States.

The FBI was able to reconstruct Ji's contacts with Intelligence Officer A and Intelligence Officer B because their contact lists were also available on Ji's iCloud database. The FBI got the necessary search warrants in March 2018 and was able to recreate what had happened. They even found messages between the intelligence officers during three visits that Ji made to China. At one point, Officer B texted Officer A (presumably Xu) telling him that Ji would be arriving in Nanjing's South Station on high speed train G203 at 22:37 (10:37 p.m.) Xu's methodology was similar to what he used in the GE case in upstate New York—inviting potential sources of stolen information to meet with him in China.

The intelligence officers asked Ji to obtain background checks from Internet-based groups such as Spokeo and Intelius on eight U.S. citizens born in Taiwan or China who were working in or had recently retired from the science and technology field, including several in aerospace. Only individuals with American-based credit cards can buy these background checks so Ji, who possessed the right credit cards, proceeded and then forwarded the information to Officer A, pretending in an email that they were "midterm test questions."

It seems that this is the pattern of how MSS finds ethnic Chinese working in American companies. The authorities don't know in advance where Chinese researchers are going to end up. They need to locate them after the fact and decide which of them are approachable.

In 2016, before the FBI started investigating, Ji enlisted in the U.S. Army Reserves as an E4/Specialist under the Military Accessions Vital to the National Interest program (MAVNI.) This allowed foreign nationals with vital skill sets to serve in the U.S. military and obtain citizenship rights. Ji lied on standardized application forms about his contacts with Chinese intelligence and then subsequently lied about it to Army investigators. It is not known what he might have done for MSS during this time in the Army Reserves, only that he lied about his contacts. An undercover agent ultimately tripped him up.

We do not know what the ultimate objective was. The MSS could have been seeking to place an electrical engineer in the heart of the U.S. Army's communications systems.

Are there more cases? Campbell, the former FBI official, declined to comment on the Joey Chun case, but he likened it to that of Richard Hanssen, who betrayed the FBI and his nation by funneling secrets to the Soviets for 15 years before he was captured in 2001. That was seen as one of the most devastating espionage cases in the agency's history. It seems there is a broader challenge from the Chinese government than just the two cases—Chun and Ji—that have been made public. "There is definitely a threat to the intelligence community, to the military and to law enforcement that the wrong types of individuals could join them to facilitate the goals and objectives of our adversaries or terrorist groups," Campbell told me. "That's an area that all those agencies need to be cognizant of, and do their best to build their recruiting and hiring and assessment programs to prevent those sort of individuals from infiltrating the organization. Because it could certainly cause grave damage. That is definitely a threat that they are attuned to and something at the federal level they are working on all the time."

Many agencies are developing or expanding their "insider threat" programs. Over the past 10 to 15 years, "the intelligence community's agencies have expanded the reviews that occur with respect to their employees' background, including a deep scope financial review and having employee assistance programs to identify when employees might be vulnerable and are going through challenging personal situations," Campbell said.

Clearly, it is a major concern. The challenge is not so much that implanted Chinese agents could cause an American government agency to do something that betrays U.S. interests. It is that the agents could provide the Chinese government with deep insights into the American decision-making system and help it anticipate what a particular U.S. agency or military branch might do. The ability to understand an antagonist's capabilities and strategies provides an enormous advantage, as Sun Tzu understood only too well.

* * *

Planting or recruiting Chinese agents inside American institutions is not the only tool being used against them. Chinese government hackers have been so aggressive against the U.S. Navy that its operational ability against Chinese forces in trouble spots such as the South China Sea may have been compromised or may one day be compromised. The *Wall Street Journal* reported in December 2018[4] that the Navy is examining the impact of a series of Chinese hacks over a period of 18 months against the Navy itself, as well as contractors and subcontractors—and even universities working on secret weapons projects for the Navy.

"Attacks on our networks are not new, but attempts to steal critical information are increasing in both severity and sophistication," Navy Secretary Richard Spencer wrote in an internal memo reviewed by the *Journal*. The hackers have been stealing so much data about such subjects as ship-maintenance data that they might be able to evaluate the battle-readiness of certain vessels. Private researchers have linked the attacks to a Chinese government hacking unit, known as Temp.Periscope or Leviathan. Like other hacking groups, it uses email phishing schemes to break into computer systems.

This data breach, combined with APT10's seizure of the personal information of 100,000 Navy personnel and hacks against smaller defense subcontractors, as described in Chapter One, suggest that the Chinese party-state has made a special target of the Navy. Its ships, after all, are the ones challenging China's right to claim sovereignty in the South China Sea where it has built military bases on previously uninhabited atolls. If the Navy is using servers that contain the secret PLA chip, as described by *Business Week*, that is another window of vulnerability.

"If you think about the types of military contingencies that China is likely to worry about the most, a conflict with the United States over Taiwan has got to be at or near the top of the list," former NSC cyber official Grotto told me. "China would assess the U.S. Navy's role in that conflict as pivotal. Understanding the capabilities and vulnerabilities of the U.S. Navy is likely high intelligence priority for them."

What's remarkable is that the Navy left itself so vulnerable. "It's extremely hard for the Defense Department to secure its own systems," Tom Bossert, a former homeland security advisor, was quoted by the *Journal* as saying. "It's a matter of trust and hope to secure the systems of their contractors and subcontractors." But trust and hope are not keeping the Chinese out. The Navy Chief of Information's office received my request for comment but said it would need Department of Defense approval before responding, which was not forthcoming.

The Pentagon as a whole appears to be as filled with opportunities for hackers. The Pentagon's own Inspector General weighed in in January 2019 with a report concluding that there are hundreds of vulnerabilities in the Pentagon's Information Technology infrastructure, leaving it vulnerable to bad actors.[5] The emphasis of the report was on the Pentagon's ability to pay its vendors and manage other financial transactions.

But it extended beyond just dollars and cents to overall practices. The audit revealed "significant control deficiencies" that prevented officials from identifying when accidental or unauthorized changes were made to databases and applications (meaning software programs). It also failed to monitor sensitive user activities, limit access to critical systems and revoke users' access once they left the Pentagon. So payments could be lost or stolen, but more broadly, "critical operations, such as those supporting national defense and emergency services, could be disrupted through weak IT controls." That's a perfect environment for Chinese government hackers although there was no specific mention of them. Of the three main branches of the military, the Navy was responsible for the largest number of vulnerabilities.

* * *

Again, the question of reciprocity looms. American agencies appear to have made some progress in improving their intelligence capabilities, as seen in the arrest of the MSS's Xu in Brussels. "Being able to apprehend someone at this level indicates the significance of the U.S. government's ability and its allies to use their intelligence collection capabilities and informants, probably Humint (Human Intelligence) and maybe electronic surveillance, to identify someone at that high level who was involved in the theft of classified information," former FBI official Campbell told me. "To track his movements, they were potentially tracking his communications through his electronic devices. Putting that together and having probable cause for a warrant for arrest and then arresting him in a third country, that speaks well of the U.S. capabilities to identify, target and apprehend someone at this level."

But that was a rare victory. The National Security Agency doubtlessly probes Chinese systems as Edward Snowden revealed, but it's difficult to imagine that it is on the same scale as what the Chinese party-state is doing inside the United States. Similarly, if the Central Intelligence Agency had many key intelligence operatives working in China, we might be able to argue that the mutual penetration of each other's decision-making apparatuses is somehow stabilizing. There is little chance that either side could be surprised because the intelligence operatives would be able to signal to their respective governments that a major decision or action was about to be taken.

But the MSS was able to dismantle the CIA's entire spy network inside China, one of the worst American intelligence failures in years. FBI agents arrested Jerry Chun Shing Lee, 53, in January 2018 for taking money from two Chinese intelligence officers and revealing information about the identities of CIA officers and informants.[6] Lee, who was born in Hong Kong and then obtained U.S. citizenship, had worked for the CIA from 1994 to 2007 as a case officer, meaning he recruited spies. After he left the agency, he moved from the United States to Hong Kong with his family.

Two intelligence officers from the MSS approached him in 2010 in Shenzhen, the Chinese city just across the Hong Kong border. They gave him $100,000 and said they would take care of him "for life" if he cooperated. They provided him with email addresses so that he could communicate covertly with them, which he did at least through 2011.

When the Chinese government shut down the CIA's operations, killing or imprisoning 18 to 20 informants,[7] the CIA started to work with the FBI to figure out what happened. The FBI lured Lee back to the United States in 2012 as part of an unspecified intelligence operation. Agents searched his belongings and found notebooks containing details about CIA operations and the identities of officers and informants. The agency allowed him to leave the United States in hopes that they could obtain further information about his activities, which is why they did not arrest him until January 2018. He pled not guilty and faces trial.

The CIA itself will not comment, of course, and it may have been able to recover somewhat from the collapse of its China network, but a careful observer cannot escape the conclusion that the Chinese government has many more ears and eyes established in U.S. institutions than the Americans do in China. One obvious reason is that the United States does not have a large population of Americans who have permanently migrated to China and penetrated deeply into Chinese institutions. There are tens of thousands of Americans living in China, and many speak Chinese well, but they are held at arm's length and have little chance of glimpsing China's internal decision-making mechanisms.

A final reason American intelligence agencies have not been able to penetrate, as well as they might have been expected to, is a giant hack China's government carried out in 2015 on the U.S. government's security clearance files of more than 22 million American officials, military personnel, contractors and intelligence officers. Those files were located in the Office of Personnel Management. Campbell, the former FBI official, was one of the victims. "Privately, American intelligence officials concluded that the Chinese were assembling a giant database of who worked with whom, and on what, in the American national security sphere, and were applying 'big data' techniques to analyze the information," David E. Sanger and Steven Lee Myers wrote in *The New York Times* in December 2018.[8] "The CIA could not move some officers to China, for fear their cover had been blown."

Another major hack of Marriott's data, believed to have emanated from the MSS, added to the impression that the Chinese have created an enormous "lake" of data about Americans and American officials, Sanger and colleagues reported a few days later. In the Marriott hack, attackers obtained personal details of nearly 400 million guests of Marriott's Starwood division, including credit card information and passport numbers. In 2017, the cyber villains got away with the personal information of 145 million Americans in the Equifax attack.

It does not appear that the Chinese are obtaining personal information for the purpose of conducting commercial fraud. Rather, the intent seems strategic. Experts say such a vast trove of personal details would help the Chinese root out any American spies in China and also keep track of which Chinese or Chinese-Americans are in touch with U.S.

intelligence agencies inside the United States. What is the party-state doing with entire databases? "That's the million dollar question," Grotto, formerly of the National Security Council, told me. The databases would have to be "groomed" before an analyst could cross-reference them, meaning picking out details about a single individual from multiple databases, he said.

That's not easy but it's possible and American Big Data experts have been doing it for years. "We can speculate based on what we know about the capabilities of data scientists in the private sector," Grotto continued. "Having that much data allows the analyst to spot trends. It enables the analyst to draw out patterns or anomalies. For example, counter-intelligence investigations are hard because all the parties involved go to great lengths to keep themselves secret. But those relationships can't exist without some form of communication and probably some exchange of information and money or rewards. If you can put together comprehensive data pictures of people, you'll be more likely to be able to identify 'tells' that humans cannot identify."

FireEye's Porter, the former CIA official, believes the cyber penetrations of U.S. government and civilian institutions has had a corrosive effect on Americans' faith in them. "Failure to act is effectively choosing to cede control not only of cyberspace but of domestic governing legitimacy," he wrote in a blog.[9] "By attacking citizens and exploiting bureaucratic and strategic failures, cyber adversaries will eventually call into question both the legitimacy and ability of the U.S. government to do its job."

I don't think the Chinese will be able to use data mining tools to predict what the American government will do, because decision-making is so complex and involves so many variables. Plus, people come and go as part of a revolving door effect. But the fact that the Chinese government may be creating an enormous database of U.S. officials as well as a cross-section of the U.S. population speaks volumes about the imbalance in intelligence capabilities between Washington and Beijing and about the ability of our most important institutions to withstand multi-faceted assaults by China's party-state.

7   The Control of Opinion Platforms

There's an old folk adage about a frog and hot water. If a pot of water is boiling and you throw a frog into the water, it will immediately jump out and escape. But if you put a frog in a pot of warm water, and gradually increase the heat, the frog won't notice. It will be cooked.

At a time when there is so much evidence that China is engaged in activities in the United States that threaten our values and interests, why have so few Americans noticed and reacted? Why is there no groundswell of public opinion, as there was after the Soviets launched Sputnik of after the Japanese attacked Pearl Harbor?

One reason is the incremental, long-term nature of China's technology-acquisition actions and efforts to penetrate American institutions. The tools our society uses to debate big issues have been muted because of China's overall ability to project "soft power" in America. It and its allies have obtained control of some policy platforms and created others, while intimidating established think tanks. Moreover, it is spending billions to carve out power in newspapers, television and movies. It has undercut the influence of American professors at universities who might criticize China by denying them visas to travel to China and wooed college presidents with donations and grants. It has developed a measure of political clout in Washington, D.C., which further discourages a robust American response. In short, it is a coordinated and sustained effort to prevent the frog from noticing that the water is getting hotter. The Russians are mere babes in the woods in comparison.

First, consider the power of opinion platforms. Hong Kong's "red billionaires," who have grown rich through their investments on the mainland and essentially declared their fealty to Beijing, now control the well-respected Asia Society (with the exception of Orville Schell's Center on U.S.-China Relations, which retains a high degree of autonomy and credibility within the Asia Society), the China Institute and the Cheung Kong Graduate School of Business. All these organizations put out publications and host events on U.S.-Chinese relations but they tend to tread softly on the real issues.

The Asia Society is now controlled by Ronnie C. Chan, who made billions of dollars in Chinese real estate deals served a six-year term as co-chair.[1] The Society recently hosted McKinsey, the consultancy, in an event describing the profit-making opportunities in serving, at the time, 731 million Chinese Internet users. No mention was made of how the Chinese government was seeking to turn the Internet into a tool of control, rather than free expression. Nor was any mention made of the challenge that China's technology ambitions represent to the United States. The audience was filled with Chinese faces. Outside voices (such as mine) were neutralized. If I had asked a critical question, I would have been heckled. I felt marginalized. Which was exactly the point.

The China Institute, located in lower Manhattan, has emerged in recent years in terms of the range and scale of its activities[2]. Its money comes from the Tung family, a prominent Hong Kong shipping and political family with a foundation. C.H. Tung, the patriarch of the family, holds a position on the Chinese People's Political Consultative Conference and attended the Communist Party Congress in 2017.[3] He has thus declared his loyalties.

Similarly, the Cheung Kong Graduate School of Business[4] is supported by the Li Ka-Shing Foundation. Li is perhaps the most famous of all the Hong Kong billionaires. The business school is billed as a private, non-profit educational institution. It is headquartered in Beijing and now has opened expensive offices in New York and London. But its events and publications are skewed against full and robust discussion of U.S.-Chinese issues.

It seems obvious that Cheung Kong is trying to create an American platform for its dean, Xiang Bing, one of China's most noted professors. He came to New York in the fall of 2018 and his school took over a ballroom in one of Manhattan's most prestigious clubs. Xiang gave a rambling talk arguing among other things that Chinese companies would have to globalize their operations to get around the wall of tariffs that President Trump seemed to be building. If a Chinese company made something in Kenya and exported it to the United States, it would not get hit with tariffs. And he defended President Xi's One Road, One Belt program, saying it was necessary to build roads and schools for poor children because he had been poor as a child. He didn't mention the multiple controversies in Sri Lanka, East Africa, Ecuador and elsewhere about the Chinese government and its state-based enterprises loaning vast sums of money, then seizing control of assets or resources when local governments could not repay. That's all occurring as part of the One Road, One Belt program to link China with Europe and much of the rest of the world. No one challenged Xiang's superficial analysis.

One of the most sophisticated techniques is to invite an American expert to appear at an event, validating the legitimacy of the platform. The Cheung Kong business school, for example, put on an event in New York on Nov. 13, roughly a week after the 2018 mid-term elections, featuring Scott Kennedy, the respected China watcher at the Center for Strategic and International Studies. The subject for the event was: "The US-China Trade Friction: What Are the Prospects for a Quick Solution?" The debate among China experts at the time was whether the U.S. and China were headed into a new "cold war" because of deepening differences across the board or whether there could be a "quick fix" to the trade deficit. "I didn't see anything nefarious in what they (Cheung Kong) were doing," Kennedy told me later. "I didn't get the idea that they were promoting any kind of policy line that was a reflection of where they are from. It just looked to me like standard type of programming that universities do all over the world." I don't argue that there was anything nefarious about it. The point is that the business school is creating a platform to play a role in shaping American opinion. Americans need to understand the power of platforms. A Cheung Kong spokeswoman declined to respond to a request for comment.

The China Institute followed up a few weeks later with a program entitled, "Will China Save the Planet?" It was based on a book of the same name by an American, Barbara Finamore. The author can be forgiven for trying to give her book a name that will attract attention and increase sales. But it seems laughable that a China-affiliated institute would promote the idea that China can save the world's environment at a time when it is, in fact, the planet's largest emitter of greenhouse gases and its construction companies are building military bases, pipelines, mines, highways and other infrastructure around the world.

China Institute President James Heimowitz sent out a fundraising letter toward the end of 2018 appealing for contributions to help the institute add 5,000 square feet of space for an auditorium and classrooms, as well as 6,000 square feet on another floor for a museum-like display that will present a glowing image of contemporary China "from digital innovation and culinary arts to cutting edge fashion and design." He made no mention of the knotty issues of Taiwan or military tensions or intellectual property theft. Clearly, Heimowitz has big plans to expand his platform in a way that will offer grand visions of China's sophistication.

In short, China's party-state and its loyalists are creating platforms or obtaining control of platforms that present a limited range of debate and seeks to intimidate other platforms they do not control. That's a second piece of the equation. Even other established, mainstream foreign policy organizations are self-influenced to go softly because they do not want to offend Chinese supporters or have their experts denied visas to travel to China, which is an important weapon that the party-state wields.

At one recent off-the-record session at a key organization, whose identity I agreed to protect, a top Chinese diplomat from the Chinese Consulate in New York, Zhao Yumin, met with some of America's top China watchers and essentially dismissed any criticism or concerns about human rights issues or governance in his country. Zhao said critics were "anti-China." Words have tremendous power to the Chinese, who have deep experience with propaganda. If you criticize some aspect of China's party-state, in today's climate you are labeled "anti-China."

Asked about President Xi's decision to extend his term indefinitely, Zhao expressed no opinion about whether the re-establishment of strong-man rule in his country was good or bad. He dismissed Western concerns about Xi's Made in China 2025 plan as just reflecting poor marketing by Chinese officials. "He didn't tell us a thing," one participant said afterward.

But participants did not confront Zhao and tell him that his presentation was an insult to their intelligence, which it was. They self-censored. This is the strategy involved in a kind of intellectual colonization—present an ideologically hard line while accepting no criticism and seeking to isolate the critics. Don't engage. Surround and isolate. Sun Tzu would have approved.

8 Projecting Media Power

The Chinese party-state has noticed the ability of the Americans over the years to project its ideals, values and culture to others through the ubiquitous U.S. media. They are seeking to follow that strategy. State-owned newspapers such as the *China Daily* distribute copies in English throughout the United States and buy space in the *Wall Street Journal, Washington Post* and *New York Times* to distribute their content. Some of the articles are interesting, but they follow the party line and do not confront any of the potentially explosive issues that the United States and China face. President Trump expressed outrage that Chinese state media bought a four-page insert in the *Des Moines Register*, alleging that it represented interference in America's political system[1]. The reality is much larger than just one newspaper. Many Americans coming into contact with China for the first time would not understand that they are being presented with propaganda.

Chinese state-owned television stations, likewise, are seeking expertise in how to project messaging in English. And China's state-run media companies are rapidly staffing up all around the world at a time when many Western news organizations have retrenched, according to a new book by Markos Kounalakis, a visiting fellow at Stanford University's Hoover Institution, a conservative think tank. His book, entitled *Spin Wars and Spy Games: Global Media and Intelligence Gathering*,[2] demonstrates that China and Russia are largely responsible for an increase in the number of "correspondents" around the world. Of course, one of their primary responsibilities is gathering intelligence about personalities and policies in their target countries, which they send home for analysis. And the "content" they produce for our consumption is skewed. At the same time, Western news organizations have been undergoing the most gut-wrenching downsizings and reductions in force seen in many decades. They are being "supplanted by non-Western organizations with state-driven agendas," Kounalakis said in an interview.[3] "The information that we're getting in the United States is becoming agenda-driven."

The U.S. Justice Department was concerned enough about the role of Xinhua (literally *new tongue*) News Agency and China Global Television Network that in September 2018 it demanded that they register as foreign agents.[4] The television network started its Washington operations in 2011 as part of an effort to create a 24-hour news channel. The immediate model was Al-Jazeera, the network established by Qatar that was well-respected for a period of time before its political agenda became too pronounced.

CGTN hired foreign consultants to help it create high-quality production standards and went live in 2012 with 75 American and 15 Chinese employees. It started with just one hour of programming, but under President Xi, the Washington bureau has now reached nearly 200 people and as of 2019 will offer 8 hours of programming a day.

It is not as hawkish and strident as Russia Today (RT), a Russian counterpart that clearly supports the Kremlin. The Chinese always seem to be at least one level more subtle than the Russians.

CGTN now has grown into a larger news organization than CNN or Fox News or the BBC, according to journalistic sources. In fact, it has become the largest network in the world in terms of numbers of employees. It broadcasts slick programming in English that can be found on YouTube. You can even watch it on your mobile device. Some of the on-air personalities are English-speaking Chinese and others are Americans hired from NBC, Bloomberg TV and Fox. It reaches 30 million American households, *The New York Times* reported[5]. It is based in a glassy office building four blocks from the White House, it added.

Its content includes rosy stories about foreign investment in China and about China's ability to keep exporting. (https://america.cgtn.com/) It is not necessarily inaccurate or misleading. Just incomplete. The reporters don't go near any of the volatile issues in Sino-American relations. A newcomer seeking to understand what all the fuss is about would view soothing, well-produced commentary on CGTN. The subtext is that everything in U.S.-Chinese relations is fine.

It also appears that CGTN will be used to promote the high-tech products that China anticipates selling in the years and decades to come. One recent segment promoted a Made-in-China medical diagnostic system that had been augmented by AI.

Xinhua is well-known as having a dual role. One is to create an editorial report. The other is to gather intelligence and send it back to Beijing.

CGTN appears to be slightly more independent than Xinhua but all the content that is broadcast in the United States still provides value to Chinese monitors at home. There may not be a direct intelligence connection, but a connection exists nonetheless. After Ma Jing, director general of CGTN America, wrote to the U.S. Department of Justice that her group enjoyed editorial independence from any Chinese party-state control, she was summoned back to Beijing to explain herself, the *Times* reported.

Again, the reciprocity issue looms. The BBC is explicitly supported by the British government and certainly projects a certain British-ness. The Voice of America, which is also government supported, seeks to spread American values about such issues as human rights around the world in multiple languages. But VOA is now a relatively minor player compared with the combination of CGTN and Xinhua.

The Chinese government also has shut down the websites of many Western news organizations in China and makes it difficult for some Western correspondents to obtain travel visas, and in some cases, revokes the visas. The vast majority of Chinese are thoroughly protected from the infection of Western news programming.

* * *

Another front in the soft power war is entertainment. Chinese investment in Hollywood studios is clearly aimed at developing movies in China and abroad that present China in a favorable light. American studios, under pressure from slower theater ticket sales and from Amazon and Netflix, are seeking Chinese cash and producing movies in China for international consumption. One in 2016 financed by Legendary Entertainment, and starring Matt Damon, was called *The Great Wall*. In it, Chinese forces atop the Great Wall fight monsters coming in from Mongolia. The Chinese are virtuous and advanced; the monsters are primitive and terrifying. Ultimately, the Chinese prevail. Americans watching the movie were in some ways being subjected to propaganda. The message of the movie could be interpreted as this: Mongolians and others from Central Asia are monsters compared with the Chinese.

Matt Damon also starred in *The Martian*, a 2015 movie backed by Chinese money. Damon, an astronaut, is stranded on Mars after a bad dust-storm and creates an agricultural system fertilized by his own feces. Ultimately, he is saved because engineers and scientists at the China National Space Administration, acting out of the goodness of their hearts, violate direct orders and make a powerful booster rocket available to rescue Damon.

The power of China's market is so strong that Beijing is able to dictate how some American movies are cast and produced, according to a story in the *Boston Globe* by Amy Qin and Audrey Carlsen in November 2018[6]. The headline of the article was, "Don't Expect a Chinese villain from Hollywood." They wrote: "Take the 2012 remake of the Cold War drama 'Red Dawn.' It depicted Chinese enemies invading a U.S. town. At least it did until the script was leaked, angering the Chinese state media. In the end, MGM spent $1 million digitally erasing evidence of the Chinese army, frame by frame, and substituting North Koreans instead."

They cited numerous other examples. "When the creators of 'Pixels' wanted to show aliens blasting a hole in the Great Wall of China, Sony executives worried that the scene might prevent the 2015 movie's release in China, leaked studio e-mails show," they wrote. "They blew up the Taj Mahal instead."

Hollywood was once sensitive to the rights of Tibetans who have been subjected to Chinese control since the 1950s. One example was the movie two decades ago, "Seven Years in Tibet," which showed Chinese soldiers brutalizing Tibetans. It was one of the top 100 grossing films of 1997. "You're not going to see something that's like 'Seven Years in Tibet' anymore," Larry Shinagawa, a professor at Hawaii Tokay International College was quoted as saying. Studios that make films critical of China risk being banned from releasing any movies in the country because President Xi is trying to make sure only Communist Party-sanctioned narratives reach either the Chinese people or international audiences.

"There is a notion that its propaganda has not worked well enough," Orville Schell, director of the Center on U.S.-China Relations, was quoted as saying. "So this is where the film industry comes in. There's a real sensitivity (on the part of the Chinese leadership) to the blockbuster power of Hollywood."

Chinese entities co-financed 41 top-grossing Hollywood films from 2013 through 2017, the article added. And China's box office market surpassed the United States in size for the first time in the first quarter of 2018 and is expected to emerge as the world's largest on an annual basis as well. Hollywood is clearly making a bet that Chinese sales and financing can help it survive, and is willing to adjust its content to win acceptance, a form of self-censorship.

Hollywood appears ready to continue its pursuit of the Chinese market even though some of its biggest stars have been banned from China for various roles they performed or for meeting Tibet's Dalai Lama. Here's a partial list of the stars and the reasons they were banned:

Jon Bon Jovi: Using an image of the Dalai Lama during a concert.

Miley Cyrus: Pulling "slant eyes" while posing for a photo.

Lady Gaga: Meeting with the Dalai Lama.

Elton John: Dedicating a performance to Chinese artist and activist Ai Weiwei.

Katy Perry: Wearing a sunflower dress, an anti-China symbol, at a performance in Taiwan.

Brad Pitt: Starring in "Seven Years in Tibet."

So far, Chinese outright acquisitions of Hollywood studios have not developed into the tsunami they once appeared to threaten. Dalian Wanda, a Chinese company, acquired the AMC cinema chain in 2012, followed in 2016 by the acquisition of the Legendary Entertainment studio. But other acquisitions failed to materialize and Wanda had to retrench because the Chinese government concluded the splashy acquisitions were excessive—and risked raising political red flags[7]. It was much better, and quieter, to exercise influence through banning "bad" actors and through the allure of the Chinese box office and access to Chinese financing. The net effect was much the same as having outright control.

* * *

One expert calls all these media and entertainment efforts to be a form of "public-opinion warfare." Dean Cheng, a senior research fellow at The Heritage Foundation in Washington, explained the concept in testimony before the Senate Judiciary Committee in December 2018.[8] "Essentially, the objective of public-opinion warfare is to establish the terms of the debate and define the parameters of coverage," Cheng said. "By presenting one's message first, the PLA (People's Liberation Army) expects to shape all others' views of a conflict. Thus, the Chinese side can underscore the justice and necessity of its operations, better display national strength, exhibit the superiority of its forces, and shake an opponent's will to resist. By contrast, adversaries must overcome the ideas that are already planted and taking root by Chinese public-opinion warfare efforts."

He continued: "Therefore, in a very real way, Chinese decision makers see public-opinion warfare as being waged even in peacetime, as part of the larger effort to shape peoples' perceptions of the PRC. There is a constant effort to influence audiences to accept China's narrative and perceptual framework."

So placing an advertising insert in the *Des Moines Register* is about more than just trying to shape a political contest in one state. It is part of a massive effort, costing hundreds of millions of dollars, to shape America's perception of China while preventing American ideas from reaching the Chinese population.

9 The Struggle for Academic Freedom

Andrew Nathan, a professor at Columbia University, is one of America's foremost Sinologists, having written countless books and articles that reflect deep expertise. But ever since he helped translate internal Chinese government documents about the Tiananmen Square massacre into English in 2001, with co-author and fellow academic Perry Link, he has been denied a visa to go to China to attend conferences or conduct academic research. The party-state has banned all mentions of the June 1989 massacre in textbooks, in the news media, and on the Internet. Many young Chinese people in their 20s have never heard of the massacre, so rigorous has the censorship been.

Nathan's troubles with the authorities started in 1995 with the book, *The Private Life of Chairman Mao*. It was in Chinese and was brought out of China by persons unknown. But Nathan was able to authenticate it and write an introduction for an English-language version. Later that year, "I was invited to participate in a delegation to visit China," Nathan described to me. "But the Chinese said Nathan could not come because I had insulted the great leader Mao." The trip was cancelled.

The Mao book helped earn Nathan a reputation as someone in the United States who could authenticate and translate sensitive Chinese documents. So in 2001, other Chinese-language documents emerged about the Tiananmen Square massacre in which thousands of protesting students were gunned down. The "Tiananmen papers" described how different factions of the Chinese government disagreed on how to handle the protesters until paramount leader Deng Xiaoping made the decision to send in the army, "killing the chicken to scare the monkey," meaning the rest of the Chinese people. "The Tiananmen papers were not just a criticism of the Chinese government—in Chinese eyes, they constituted a breach of state security," Nathan explained. "I wasn't in China when I received these documents. Nor did I seek them out or weasel them out. I was in New York and a person came along and asked me to take them." But nonetheless Nathan was seen as having spilled state secrets.

As soon as the book came out, a spokesman for the Chinese government denounced it. "I knew I would be banned for that project and that has been the case," Nathan said. "Twice people in China have told me they had gotten permission to invite me and I should apply for a visa. In both cases, when I applied, the Consulate General in New York was afraid to issue it without approval from the Ministry of Foreign Affairs. And the foreign ministry didn't feel comfortable enough to issue the visa, so I never went."

No one on the American side knows how many American professors and think tank experts are on China's banned list, but several told me they believe the number is growing. One reason we don't know more is that American experts who cannot obtain visas do not want to advertise the fact because it might undermine their academic legitimacy. If they can't go to China, how can they be a China expert? Still others hope that if they remain silent and don't anger Chinese authorities anew, they will be able to lobby the government to start issuing visas to them again.

Getting banned did not destroy Nathan's career because he already had tenure and his specialty is China's foreign affairs, meaning what China's party-state is doing outside of China. "I can go places and meet people from

China," Nathan explained. "By being banned, I have had a different kind of experience getting to know lots of Chinese people from another angle, as a person they trust. I think I've learned some good things and it has enriched my ability to analyze China by being banned. I've gotten positive things as well as negative things from the experiences I've had."

But the symbolism to others of what happened to Nathan and Link is clear. Minky Worden of Human Rights Watch, who has taught a graduate level class at Columbia's School of International and Political Affairs, told me she considers the treatment of Nathan and Link to be part of the party-state's conscious long-term strategy of suppressing academic freedom in the United States if it involves criticism. "What are the effects of not allowing Perry Link or Andy Nathan, two preeminent scholars of contemporary China, to go to China?" she asks. "If you have spent decades studying China and the Chinese language, denying them a visa cuts off their access to the thing they know the most about. It has the effect of 'killing the chicken to scare the monkey.' No other academic wants to be cut off from the thing they've spent decades learning about. It also shuts up the specific people who know too much and expose your dirty linen. It's not in isolation—the treatment of Perry Link and Andy Nathan is a warning to all other academics."

She is also concerned about the proliferations of Confucius Institutes at American universities. The Chinese government pays to support the institutes at about 100 American universities and colleges that purport to support U.S.-Chinese cultural relations, but they may have the effect of suppressing debate, not encouraging it. The institutes are run by the Hanban, a unit of the PRC's Ministry of Education. The Hanban signs confidential contracts with the American universities and high schools to create China-study programs and the contracts specify that neither party will do anything that violates Chinese law, according to the blockbuster report, "Chinese Influence & American Interests: Promoting Constructive Vigilance," released in late November 2018.[1] It was written by America's top China watchers and was co-led by the above-mentioned Schell and Larry Diamond, a senior fellow at the Hoover Institution at Stanford University. According to them, the Hanban, meaning the Ministry of Education, is able to prohibit discussion at its Confucius Institutes of sensitive issues such as Taiwan or Tibet or the Uighurs in Xinjiang Province, who are being subjected to mass arrests and forced labor.

The FBI has investigated some of the Confucius Institutes. One university, Texas A&M, said it would terminate its agreement to host a Confucius Institute in response to the urging of two congressmen who described the institutes as threats to national security.[2] A handful of other universities have followed suit.

Worden blames university presidents and administrators for their "stunning and egregious naïveté" in taking the Chinese government's money without insuring that their intellectual and academic independence are fully guaranteed. "Chinese people who go abroad have aspirations," she explained. "Everyone carries knowledge of what happened to their grandparents or great grandparents in the Cultural Revolution (when millions died in political struggles.) No one wants to return to that. There is a hope that education is the way out of the economic and cultural darkness. But the Chinese government has recognized that the U.S. educational system, because it is not very well-informed about contemporary China, is a perfect place to exert its political pressures and nefarious means of obtaining information."

If American universities give the Hanban the opportunity to make secret agreements, "why wouldn't they?" Worden asked. "That's our fault. It is incumbent on intellectual organizations to know the conditions under which they are operating. Chinese government policy is not a secret. It's all knowable. It's been in front of everyone for decades. University leaders are saying, 'You're bringing us the ability to train people in Mandarin? Sign us up. If you want the contract to be secret, sign us up. We're not going to be able to talk about Taiwan or Tiananmen? No worries. Sign us up.'"

Worden believes the Confucius institutes and the web of agreements they have signed with American universities has "created an enabling environment for the theft of intellectual property. University professors don't report what they are seeing in the behavior of their students."

Other voices on China's effort to shape American universities say the onus is on academic leaders to do a better job of resisting Chinese government pressures. Robbie Barnett, who recently retired after leading Columbia's Modern Tibetan Studies program for 19 years, has not been able to get a visa to China or Tibet, his major area of study, for 10 years. He has tried several times. But he places the burden of maintaining American academic freedom squarely on the shoulders of American university leaders. "Americans deny visas all the time," Barnett, who is British, told me. "Every country does it. Americans probably do it more than China and much more randomly. The Chinese are very, very targeted. They try not to do it too much. They select certain key people to intimidate the rest of us, to make us self-censor.

"The major issue is why our universities don't take a position on their scholars being banned," Barnett continued. "They should absolutely be saying if you ban Andrew Nathan or Perry Link, we are not going to cooperate with you." He

said not a single university has done that. At least some
universities may be valuing the China connection and
associated revenues more than they care to fight for the
academic freedom of their professors.

* * *

Chinese diplomats based in the United States do make
direct approaches to American universities in an effort to
discourage events or speakers that stray from the official
Communist Party line, according to a 2018 report from the
highly respected Wilson Center in Washington, D.C.[3] The
center, chartered by Congress as the official memorial to
President Woodrow Wilson, is a key nonpartisan policy forum.
Anastasya Lloyd-Damnjanovic authored the study and
conducted interviews with more than 180 people to talk about
events of the two previous decades.

Aside from its embassy in Washington, the Chinese
government maintains consulates in New York City, Chicago,
San Francisco, Los Angeles and Houston, putting its diplomats
in easy reach of many top universities. They presumably learn
about campus events from Chinese students or professors.
"PRC diplomats have, since at least the early 1990s, made
official expressions of displeasure to American universities for
hosting certain speakers and events," the report said.

It added: "The findings suggest a worrisome trend in
which faculty, students, administrators, and staff across a range
of disciplines within American universities are encountering
pressure to align their academic activities with PRC political
preferences. Such pressure may limit critical discourse about
China on campus, harming the learning environment for other
students from the PRC, the United States, and third countries.

If the infringements associated with PRC actors become widespread, faculty, students, administrators, and staff in the United States may find themselves acclimatizing to the PRC's domestic censorship standards." In other words, China's diplomats—so far, in a limited number of cases—are seeking to impose the same type of censorship that the party-state uses back in China.

How to respond remains controversial. The Wilson Center report suggests the possibility of expelling Chinese diplomats who interfere in academic affairs. But Barnett said the Chinese party-state's efforts are to be expected. "We shouldn't be attacking China for trying to exert its influence. That's what governments are paid to do, what their diplomats do," Barnett argued. "The question is whether China is effective in subverting the basic principles of academic life. The question is whether we have resistance to it."

In some ways, Chinese authorities seem to place a higher emphasis on American universities than America's own political leaders do. I asked Nathan why. "Our universities are the best in the world still," he explained. "The whole STEM part of it is very important in terms of sending students and visiting scholars over here to just learn and go back with those skills and to some extent steal technology."

The Chinese also have a tradition of respect for intellectuals. "They believe that professors have substantial influence over government policy," Nathan continued. "I guess we have some influence. I feel in my own case by teaching and seeing my students go on to be in the government and through occasional consultations in Washington, through my media work or non-profit work, I am a voice on policy. I know a lot of people in the government. But I don't think we're quite as important as they (the Chinese government) think we are."

President Xi has told television network CGTN and by implication, everyone involved in China's propaganda activities, that he wants them to "tell China stories well" to the rest of the world.[4] "Our big educational system is one of the places along with the media that the China story is told," Nathan said. "They very sincerely feel that people don't understand in the West how good China is and how legitimate China's aspirations are, and that there are a lot of biased critics. They want to influence that."

* * *

Aside from the revenue that American universities derive from the 350,000 Chinese students in the United States, about 14 of them have opened campuses in China in cooperation with Chinese universities, *China Daily*, an official newspaper, reported in January 2018.[5] New York University, Duke, and the University of California at Berkeley are the most prominent. That could be a great avenue to encourage American students to go to China to study but it seems that Chinese students represent the vast majority of enrollees. They can obtain a degree from a U.S. university without having to travel to and live in the United States. To these students, "it's a convenient and cost-effective way to acquire a U.S. degree without studying abroad," an official at San Francisco State University was quoted as saying. Statistics are not available but it would seem clear that these 14 American universities are enjoying a stream of revenue from having campuses in China.

The Chinese government and private interests who wish to curry favor with it have established a variety of academic exchange programs and travel programs to the mainland. Plus, the Chinese are an increasing source of donations to American universities. The great risk, of course, is that universities allow their voices to be muted because of a web of interactions and dependencies. "The Chinese government has demonstrated a penchant for turning to these collaborations as points of leverage when U.S. universities have hosted the Dalai Lama (of Tibet) or held other events deemed politically sensitive or offensive to the Chinese government," the Chinese Influence & American Interests report said.

"In such instances, existing collaborative exchange programs have been suspended or put on hold, planned visits of university administrators have been canceled, programs between university institutes and centers have been suspended, and Chinese students wishing to study at these U.S. institutions have been counseled to go elsewhere," it continued. "Such punitive actions resulting from campus visits by the Dalai Lama have been taken against Emory University, the University of Maryland, the University of California–San Diego, and others."

It concluded: "Such cases establish a worrying precedent of Chinese intrusion into American academic life. The message from China to U.S. universities is clear: Do not transgress the political no-go zones of the Chinese Communist Party or government, or you will pay a price."

The great risk, of course, is that intimidation of outspoken Western professors combined with all the economic benefits that universities are reaping from Chinese sources will cause university presidents to conclude, as have some Hollywood studios, that it is better to reap the economic benefits and bolster their own institutions rather than taking leading roles in the great debate about China.

Critics put forth two examples: The Chinese party-state allowed Nobel Peace Prize-winning Liu Xiaobo, a renegade intellectual, to die in prison in 2017 under guard rather than allow him to seek treatment in the West. Liu was described as a mild-mannered professor who helped save hundreds of student lives during the Tiananmen massacre by negotiating their departure from the area. The outside world, including diplomats and academics, were largely silent about his treatment. "His dying in state custody without much of a peep from the international community is an example of how devoid of principles and values our China policy has become," Worden of Human Rights Watch says. "The small number of people who were prepared to defend him and his wife tells you about the failings to defend basic principles and how China has trained generations of diplomats and academics to shut up in the face of abuses."

Another top China watcher, Jerome Cohen, in September 2018 launched a campaign against China's intimidation of Western experts regarding a second human rights issue[6]. Cohen, who teaches at New York University, teamed up with Kevin Carrico, a scholar at Australia's Macquarie University, to highlight the Chinese government's treatment of an estimated 1 million Uighurs in its far western province of Xinjiang. According to multiple news reports, the Chinese government has split up families and placed many adults in what it calls vocational training centers. But news reports are persistent in demonstrating that the real intent of the camps is to break the Uighurs' commitment to Islam and their own traditions.

Scholars who study China were largely silent, at least in the initial stages as media report after media report spotlighted the issue. The reason? They feared not being able to obtain visas to travel to China. "The global response to these developments has been muted," the two professors said in a joint statement signed by more than 100 other scholars. "Those who stand up and speak out openly against these practices may face the wrath of a rising power that is determinedly hostile to criticism."

As with so many other aspects of its soft power campaign, the Chinese party-state is relying on many different carrots and sticks to pursue its goals. Wealthier elite universities such as Columbia can resist Beijing's blandishments, but other smaller state universities and smaller private colleges—in some cases facing declining state funding and falling enrollments by American students—may not be as fortunate. It seems clear that the Chinese government's mix of incentives and disincentives has had at least some impact in terms of muting what I believe should be a major topic on college campuses—how should the United States respond to an increasingly powerful authoritarian state that does not respect the concept of intellectual or academic freedom on our own shores?

10 Exporting Chinese-Style Control Systems

Rose Tang, a native of Sichuan Province, was a 20-year-old college student in Beijing, when she heard about students gathering in Tiananmen Square to demand democratic rights. Always a rebel, Rose was in the square when the Chinese army tanks and troops attacked the students on June 4, 1989. She was one of the last group of still-living protesters to leave the area, crawling over an army tank, just below its machine gun barrel, so that the soldiers inside could not see her. Minutes later, she was interviewed by CNN and ended up working for the network for two years.

Today, Tang is an American citizen and an activist who campaigns against the Chinese party-state. "To remain silent is a crime," she told me. She traveled to Dharamshala, India, the headquarters of exiled Tibetans, to meet the Dalai Lama in 2014, making her a rare Chinese crusader for Tibetan rights. She also traveled to Hong Kong to camp out with protesters in the so-called Umbrella Movement, who were demanding independence for the former British colony from China. Back in New York City, where she lives, she posts a steady stream of attacks on different aspects of what China does in the world on social media. "I want to be seen," she said. "I want to make people think. I speak for people who cannot be heard. I do what others cannot do."

Tang is one of many Chinese dissidents and activists who have taken shelter in the United States. Except, there isn't really true shelter. You're a free person, I told her. "No, I'm not. They're watching me," she said, referring to the Chinese government. She assumes that all her electronic communications, even if they are purely domestic within the United States, are being intercepted by Chinese intelligence agencies.

She can't be sure just how she is being monitored electronically but she knows she's a target because she gets hacked on a regular basis. Google once contacted her to warn her that someone else was trying to log into her Gmail account. And a steady stream of government agents attempt to enter her life. They pose as new Chinese dissidents or even Tibetan and Uighur dissidents, and attempt to befriend her, hoping to tap into her network of friends and allies. "They tell me elaborate stories about their plight and how they escaped," Tang said.

One famous dissident asked her to take care of a new arrival from the mainland who identified herself as another dissident. "Once when she came to my house for dinner, she asked to stay overnight when she didn't have to," Tang recalled, "That's when I started to get suspicious." Another woman agent claimed to be an independent film maker but asked detailed, personal questions about Tang's job prospects. What gave her away as a spy was that she had lots of money. "She bought a house in Princeton and she was going to be here only two or three years," she said, "I certainly can't afford that. That was so blatant."

So the joke among Tang's circle of Chinese friends is, "How do you recognize an agent when you meet one?" Answer: "See if they bought a house."

Tang has cut off communications with her parents and a sister and all her friends in China in hopes of sparing them harassment by Chinese authorities. A kind of shadow war is still raging between the Chinese government and Tiananmen survivors around the world. Families of Tang's dissident friends back in China have been harassed or arrested or put on exit bans, meaning they cannot leave the country. Tang certainly can never return. "I have to pay a hefty price for what I do," she said.

It seems such a basic principle: any foreigner legally in the United States gets to enjoy the freedoms we enjoy, particularly so if they are on the path toward citizenship or already have become citizens. At the same time, they are bound by our laws and no other nation's. That's a concept called sovereignty.

But the Chinese party-state does not respect that principle. It targets not only Chinese dissidents in the United States, but also the 350,000 students at American universities. And it tries to draw adult Chinese-Americans into unification societies in different American cities, making them part of the party-state's "United Front" effort to advance its interests inside the United States.

Chinese authorities try to control the students through Chinese Student and Scholar Associations (CSSAs). According to a report from the conservative Hudson Institute, the Chinese government's embassy in Washington and five consulates in the United States support and manage the CSSAs.[1] The local chapters, concentrated at universities with large Chinese student populations, provide information-gathering and ideological support for the Chinese government.

They are on the watch for "problem" students to emerge. When a student named Yang Shuping delivered a commencement speech at the University of Maryland upon her graduation, she praised the "fresh air of free speech" compared with the political environment in China. The Maryland CSSA sharply rebuked her and a Chinese embassy official encouraged other CSSAs to follow suit against any other would-be critics.[2]

Another report has emerged at the University of
Georgia where a Chinese student and activist, Sulaiman Gu,
told Radio Free Asia that Chinese police tried to recruit him
to spy on other Chinese students.[3] "According to my
understanding, you wouldn't be taken straight to prison the
moment you came back to China," a secret police officer tells
Gu in a recording of a recent phone call shared with the radio
outlet. "But seeing as you are pretty active and you have said
various things that have had a negative impact on the country
and the government, you are definitely a person of interest."
The voice specifically asked Gu for information about any pro-
democracy groups that Chinese students were involved in.

A story in *Foreign Policy* magazine was highly revealing.[4]
In May 2018, the magazine ran a story by Qiu Zhongsun,
which it acknowledged was a pen name to conceal the real
identity of the Chinese student who wrote the article. Qiu was
at the University of California in San Diego when President
Xi declared that he would not name a successor, effectively
making him president for life. Qiu put up a poster of Xi in
the student lounge with three words written across his face:
Not My President.

Qiu concealed his own identity when he put up the
picture by wearing a hoodie and waiting until late at night to
put it up with a friend. He and his friends also started a Twitter
campaign called #NotMyPresident and encouraged like-
minded Chinese students at other universities to protest.
Chinese students at some 30 universities outside of China took
part.

But they knew that their job prospects back in China
could suffer if their identities became known, and worse.
"Chinese authorities have also been known to harass the
families of outspoken Chinese students abroad, to interrogate

Chinese returnees, or, in extreme cases, even kidnap Chinese abroad and force them back to China," Qiu wrote.

To avoid being monitored, the students avoided WeChat messages, a Chinese messaging application that the Chinese government monitors closely. They bought anonymous burner phones, which are prepaid and cannot be tracked, and used encrypted messaging applications backed by Facebook. But Chinese censors, operating from China, apparently went on the hunt for the rebellious students. "We faced a barrage of phishing attempts," Qiu wrote. "Every day, we received dubious password reset requests in the inboxes of each campaign-related account: Twitter, Facebook, Gmail, even the Dropbox account we used to host our posters for download." Some of the messages said that a particular account had been blocked and urged the students to click on an "unlock" button, which would have allowed the censors to penetrate their systems and learn their identities.

Qiu concluded: "For mainland Chinese like myself, the oppression we face at home follows us abroad. The Chinese Communist Party has learned how to project its regime of surveillance and coercion deep inside the borders of liberal democracies."

* * *

The Chinese party-state also seeks to organize adult ethnic Chinese in America through the National Association for China's Peaceful Unification based in Washington, according to research by Bethany-Allen Ebrahimian published in The Daily Beast[5]. She has done the best journalistic work on this piece of China's influence efforts. This organization describes itself as a non-profit for Chinese-Americans dedicated to the eventual unification of China with Taiwan. It has more than 30 chapters in cities such as San Francisco, Chicago, Houston, New York and Washington. Diplomats from China's consulates openly support these chapters, which may engage on issues other than Taiwan such as Tibet, Hong Kong, and China's maritime expansion into the South China Sea.

Ebrahimian described how all this is part of the Communist Party's United Front strategy, which it has long employed to create coalitions of different groups to help achieve the party's ultimate goals. "These days, the United Front operations sometimes resemble the CIA's soft attempts to buy off, co-opt or coerce influential community leaders," she wrote. "Sometimes it functions like a booster club for pro-party locals, or like the advocacy group trying to sway public opinion. Sometimes it works in concert with China's traditional intelligence agencies, such as the Ministry of State Security, to gather information or to apply pressure. And United Front networks may sometimes play a role in facilitating intellectual property theft and soft intelligence collection, though that role isn't always clear."

Ebrahimian appeared to be present for the elevation of a Chinese-American woman to become president of the National Association for China's Peaceful Unification in Washington D.C. "He (Helen) Xiaohui posed for a photo with the previous president, who was symbolically handing over an object to her. Presiding over the January 13 handover was Li Kexin, a high-profile minister at the Chinese Embassy in Washington. Li stood between the two, a hand on each of their backs.

"No matter the time, no matter the situation, the Chinese government and 1.4 billion Chinese people will always have your back," Li said. "I believe that this new cohort of leadership will continue to unite the power of overseas Chinese, and hold high the banners of anti-independence (for Taiwan) and peaceful unification."

It's difficult to document precise cases where the Chinese associations and their United Front strategies have been effective in swaying American policy-making. But the Chinese government is trying to use these organizations as if they were on the mainland. Government officials don't recognize that Chinese-Americans have a primary loyalty to the United States. "While Americans are quick to label any wariness of communist parties as McCarthyism, and while the potential for racial stereotyping is real, the Chinese Communist Party's United Front Work Department and International Liaison Department—two of the main bodies overseeing such exchanges—are in fact active and well-resourced and determined," the Chinese Influence & American Interests report concluded. "No mainland Chinese organization in the United States—corporate, academic, or people-to-people—is free of Beijing's control, even if it is not formally part of the United Front."

It's as if there is a Bamboo Curtain—on our own soil—and we cannot penetrate what happens behind it.

* * *

Chinese living in North America, of whatever age, may be harassed by Chinese authorities if they become too politically active, as the Rose Tang case demonstrates. But there are others. The National Post of Canada in January 2018[6] told the story of one Chinese dissident in Ontario who barely raised any Canadian eyebrows with mild suggestions for reform back home. Then he went home to visit family. "Security officers shadowed him for weeks, booking hotel rooms next to his, even following him to breakfast," the newspaper wrote.

"Before he left, they also had a disturbingly direct message: Stop condemning the Chinese government to the Canadian media, or the family he had come to visit would face the consequences. 'They said if this (critical) story came out in the Canadian press, then you are responsible for the life of your relatives,' he recalls."

According to a confidential report submitted to the Canadian government, the newspaper said the case was just one example of a sweeping intimidation campaign by Chinese officials against activists in Canada. Activists in the United States face similar pressures, as in the case of Rose Tang. "In terms of effectiveness, harassing Chinese living abroad has a chilling effect on free speech within the Chinese diaspora," Yaqiu Wang, a China researcher at Human Rights Watch, told me.

If you add up all the strands, once again, of what the Chinese government is doing regarding American opinion platforms and think tanks, universities, media, and controlling and using Chinese students and Chinese-Americans, it becomes clear that it is trying to project its values into the American body politic. "China's influence activities have collectively helped throw the crucial relationship between the People's Republic of China and the United States into a worrisome state of imbalance and antagonism," the Chinese Influence & American Interests report said.

"Not only are the values of China's authoritarian system anathema to those held by most Americans, but there is also a growing body of evidence that the Chinese Communist Party views the American ideals of freedom of speech, press, assembly, religion, and association as direct challenges to its defense of its own form of one-party rule," it added.

Revealingly, the study compared the influence activities of China to those of Russia. "China is intervening more resourcefully across a wider range of sectors than Russia," it said. "By undertaking activities that have become more organically embedded in the pluralistic fabric of American life, it has gained a far wider and potentially longer-term impact."

This report is remarkable because it essentially represents a rejection of President Xi's policies by the very intellectuals, academics and diplomats who have guided America's engagement with China from the very beginning. One signatory was Winston Lord, who traveled with Henry Kissinger on the first secret trip into China to start negotiations to normalize relations and who later served as U.S. ambassador to China. Others—Orville Schell, Elizabeth Economy, Gen. Karl Eikenberry (Ret.), Bonnie Glaser, Andrew Nathan, David Shambaugh, and Ezra Vogel—are household names to anyone who has followed the U.S. role in East Asia, lo these many decades. These China-watchers were able to issue this very tough report in part because their careers are cresting or have crested. Many are in their 60s and 70s. They have nothing left to lose.

"If you think of the China (watching) community as consisting of a small number of 'panda huggers' on the fringe and a small number of hostile anti-China people on the other fringe, this group was mainstream," Nathan told me. "We don't want the U.S.-China relationship to drift into antagonism and conflict, but we no longer believe China is on the right track toward fairer economic relations and a more stable security relationship with the United States or toward converging values with the United States. It reflects disappointment and a sense that the relationship is at a dangerous turning point. We basically blame Xi Jinping.

There is disillusionment and disappointment and a dwindling hope that the relationship can get back on a stable track."

The big question is whether following generations of China watchers—who still need visas—will take positions as courageous.

11 Playing the Game in Washington

When it was revealed in April 2018 that Chinese telecommunications company ZTE had violated U.S. sanctions against Iran and North Korea, and then lied about it, the U.S. Department of Commerce banned the company from buying any American products for seven years.[1] The company was already in bad repute in Washington because of its possible role in selling phone equipment internationally that might contain a "back door" through which the Chinese military or intelligence agencies could eavesdrop on the world's communications. Without U.S. components, such as semiconductors designed by Qualcomm, ZTE would collapse.

Its solution? Acting through a U.S. subsidiary to avoid having to disclose that it was a foreign entity, it spent $1.4 million over three months to hire a prominent U.S. law firm, Hogan Lovells, and a lobbying and public relations firm, Mercury Public Affairs. An excellent article in *The New York Times* described the battle.[2] They launched a campaign to lobby the White House, Congress, the Commerce Department and the Treasury Department.

President Trump complicated matters by taking a phone call from President Xi. "In the case of ZTE, my understanding is that the key decision point wasn't ZTE's lobbying or the use of a consulting firm, but the phone call between Presidents Xi and Trump," Kennedy of CSIS told me. "Trump agreed in the phone call to change his mind without having much information at all. Most of the information about ZTE he had most likely was given to him by Xi Jinping in the phone call. After the phone call, he mentioned how many employees ZTE had, which was one of Xi's talking points."

Even after the Trump reversal, however, the battle continued. In mid-July, top lawmakers began trying to unify Senate and House versions of a military bill that contained the ban on selling U.S. products to ZTE. It was then that Hogan Lovells demonstrated its true clout by reaching out to two congressmen on the committee that was trying to come up with unified language.

"At least two members of the House-Senate committee—Senator Lindsey Graham of South Carolina and Representative Ed Royce of California, both Republicans— were featured speakers at a party hosted by Hogan Lovells celebrating the debut of the firm's newly combined lobbying and public affairs practice," the *Times* wrote.

Two days later, it emerged that the legislation drafted by the conference committee contained a watered-down version of the penalties against ZTE. Both lawmakers declined to comment.

The company paid a steep price for the deal, including a fine and having to install a new board of directors. But the net result was that a Chinese company was able to prevail in an intense political fight in Washington. "This is how #China influences our government policies," tweeted Florida Senator Marco Rubio. "They spent a small fortune lobbying Congress to drop restrictions on #ZTE and it worked."

The party-state is still in the learning stages about how to wield influence in Washington because a democracy is so fundamentally different than a one-party state. "My sense is that the China's general knowledge about the American policy process and the players has increased," Kennedy said. "They understand the role of interest groups on a day-to-day basis and in regard to elections."

One show of sophistication was the products and geographies that the Chinese choose to retaliate against after Trump imposed the first round of tariffs. The party-state clearly targeted products from regions that support Trump politically.

"But they have a long way to go before I would call them successful influencers in Washington," Kennedy added. "The most successful Chinese that operate in this town outsource their activity to American consulting firms and lobbyists as opposed to doing it themselves. I think from a Chinese government perspective, they still are a fish out of water in Washington, particularly on large public policy issues. They are very uncomfortable interacting with the American media or other parts of American civil society or members of Congress. Their language and the kinds of arguments they make don't show a strong appreciation of the audiences they're interacting with."

But they are learning how to play the game, in part by using law firms. Huawei, which is bigger and more prestigious than ZTE, cut back on its efforts to communicate with Congress in 2018 and instead turned to two law firms, Jones Day and Morgan, Lewis & Bockius, to help it fight a proposal by the Federal Communications Commission to prevent small wireless and Internet providers from using federal subsidies to buy Huawei equipment.[3]

Huawei obviously has a huge problem in Washington following the detention of its chief financial officer, Meng Wanzhou, in Vancouver at the request of American authorities.[4] They alleged that she was involved in tricking financial institutions into transactions that violated U.S. sanctions against Iran. Meng, the daughter of Huawei's founder, was awaiting extradition to the United States. The company recently dispatched Joy Tan, its head of global communications, to Washington to replace another executive and become its top representative in Washington. Tan has played a key role in the company's media relations. Whether she can fashion a winning campaign with the Trump administration remains in doubt.

* * *

Huawei is throwing its cash around in different ways. Think tanks play an essential role in Washington in doing the heavy-lifting, intellectually speaking, that policy makers then use as part of their overall decision-making process. The American Enterprise Institute and the Hudson Institute, both on the conservative end of the political spectrum, have lined up squarely on the side of those in the administration who want to get tough with China. It was at the Hudson Institute, after all, that Mike Pence delivered his denunciation of Chinese practices in October 2018.[5]

But the commentary emanating daily from the Brookings Institution has sought to downplay the need for confrontation, and one possible reason emerged in December 2018 in an opinion piece by Isaac Stone Fish in the *Washington Post*.[6] Fish described how Huawei had given hundreds of thousands of dollars to Brookings and that Brookings had written a report praising Huawei's technology.

It was in October 2017 that Brookings published a report entitled "Benefits and Best Practices of Safe City Innovation." The report concentrated on two cities—the Kenyan capital of Nairobi and the Chinese city of Lijiang. Both had implemented new policing technology, presumably using cameras and facial recognition technology.

What the report failed to mention is that Huawei provided the technology for both cities. "In other words," Fish wrote, "Brookings praised Huawei's technology in a report sponsored by Huawei." The report did acknowledge that Huawei had provided support but omitted that Huawei's technologies were used in both cities.

It turned out that Huawei gave at least $300,000 to Brookings via FutureWei Technologies, Inc., its U.S-based subsidiary, between July 2016 and June 2018. Brookings said it disclosed the gifts from Huawei and found no violations of its policies in the conduct of Darrell W. West, Brookings vice president and founding director of its Center for Technology Innovation, who wrote the report. West also traveled widely to Huawei-sponsored events in Milan, Italy, and elsewhere, where he defended Huawei against allegations that it represented a threat to U.S. telecommunication systems.

Every think tank in Washington is on the prowl at all times for new sources of funding. It's just how the game is played. But as the technological and economic interests of China and the United States collide, think tanks such as Brookings may need to contemplate what role they play in the American democracy.

* * *

A key question is whether the Chinese party-state can exploit its economic power to achieve policy goals in the United States. The economic stakes are enormous: General Motors sells more vehicles in China than it does in the United States. Intel sells more semiconductors in China than it sells in the United States. Boeing sells a quarter of all its planes in China. Apple depends on China for the manufacturing of all its iPhones. Wal-Mart and Home Depot depend on China for a vast array of products.

A fascinating test case was unfolding as I was concluding this book. Trump imposed some small tariffs on China against the advice of many American corporate leaders. Then he imposed 10 percent tariffs on $200 billion in made-in-China goods and threatened to raise those tariffs to 25 percent tariffs if a sweeping trade agreement was not reached between the two governments.

The message from the Chinese party-state to American businesses was clear: China has the power to inflict great damage on American companies as San Diego-based Qualcomm found out the hard way: the Chinese blocked its acquisition of another company, NXP, because of anti-trust concerns in the Chinese market. The government retains enormous control over companies that either buy or sell things in China. Imagine the dilemma that Apple faces with its entire production of smart phones being carried on out the mainland. Wall Street seems particularly sensitive to U.S.-China trade tensions and Trump cares about Wall Street.

So American companies tried to persuade Trump not to impose the new higher tariffs. I happen to agree that the tariffs will not address the fundamental problems in the U.S.-Chinese relationship. They will penalize consumers who have to spend more money at Wal-Mart for things made in China. It could take months or years for Wal-Mart to find and develop other suppliers for all the goods it buys in China. American companies active in China and their shareholders and employees will suffer. There will be enormous damage and no positive outcome.

So if American business persuades Trump to begin easing the trade tensions, does that mean that it has become captive to Chinese interests and is subverting the power of an American president? I think the answer is "no." They will merely have explained the reality that tariffs are not effective.

Longer-term, the question is whether American business interests choose to play a role in helping broad cross sections of Americans come to grips with the deeper technological and policy challenges the United States faces with the Chinese party-state. Heretofore, American business leaders have not been particularly visible trying to advise various levels of American governments about how to develop key technologies to compete against Chinese ambitions. Nor have they engaged with the federal government in a serious campaign to halt the digital hacking. They have concentrated on making money and meeting their quarterly profit targets, which some perceive as their only goals.

What are the implications? There are some issues where the Chinese have little chance of succeeding—Congress expanded the role of the CFIUS to scrutinize Chinese acquisitions of U.S. technology companies as well as minority investments and it toughened export control rules. But on other issues, we simply do not know whether Chinese interests will be able to shape important elements of U.S. policy, whether overtly or covertly. They are certain to try.

A key issue once again is reciprocity. If U.S. companies were able to hire Chinese lobbyists and win key battles in Beijing, we could agree that the playing field was relatively level. But the nature of decision-making in Beijing is largely inscrutable. It takes place behind closed doors. American executives have access to some Chinese officials and seek to bring pressure on the government through trade associations, chambers of commerce, and other means. But there is no chance that an American company could hire lobbyists or consultants who had served in the heart of the party-state's decision-making process.

* * *

It's important to keep adding up the strands. Examining the different avenues of China's influence operations in the United States, it becomes clear that there are many more than Americans recognize. "The model of using all the systems of Western democracies to undermine them—that's China's secret sauce," Worden of Human Rights Watch told me. "They are using the institutions of democracy to undermine them."

Consider the issue of our free press. Our newspapers accept advertising from whomever has the money, with certain limitations of course. But very few. "Look at the *People's Daily* and their massive advertising supplements that are promoting the PRC's business in *The Washington Post* and *The New York Times*," she said. "For people who can't tell the difference between an advertorial and a news story, it presents a real problem. A lot of people don't know the difference. All they know is that the advertorial looks like *The New York Times*."

The Chinese party-state has attempted to mute critical university voices and has also succeeded in prevailing upon Hollywood studios to not make movies where Chinese characters are villains, as previous chapters have chronicled. "Hollywood was punished for making the Tibetan movies," Worden says. "They killed a chicken to scare the monkey. They made examples of Hollywood actors or actresses or film companies by barring them from the Chinese market. Then no one else ever makes a film on Tibet. It's not a one-off thing. It's always a strategy. The PRC has been very good at exercising its strategy and vision over a period of decades."

It's the very porous nature of the American democracy, and the inevitable political transitions caused by elections, that allows the Chinese strategy to work. "Some of the blame for this rests with the United States," Worden says. "Successive administrations, Republican and Democratic alike, have not had a consistent policy and therefore Beijing has been able to successfully manipulate them and wait out any criticism. If you don't like the policy of the U.S. Trade Representative's office, you just wait until you have a U.S. trade representative who is open to doing and saying dumb things.

"The Chinese government approach on this is really the Long March approach," she added, referring to Mao Tse-tung's decision to lead his army and supporters on a more than 5,000-mile retreat in the mid-1930s to escape encirclement by enemy Nationalist forces. It became one of the central images of contemporary Chinese political history. "The government is saying, 'We are going to outlast everybody. We know that if you oppose us, we will eventually overrun you. You will lose your position through an election or you will leave government to make money. If we didn't bring you around while you were in office, once you are making money for a company or a think tank, we'll be able to neutralize your troublesome views through economic means.' The revolving door in U.S. foreign policy makes this especially difficult. It is a problem that generations of State Department, White House and Pentagon officials have gone out to work for consultants and think tanks. The Chinese leadership recognizes that."

The king of Wu asked Sun Wu:

"The enemy is courageous and unafraid, arrogant and reckless. His soldiers are numerous and strong. What should we do?"

Sun Wu said:

"Speak and act submissively in order to accord with their intentions. Do not cause them to comprehend (the situation) and thereby increase their indolence. In accord with the enemy's shifts and changes, submerge (our forces) in ambush to await (the moment). Then do not look at their forward motion, nor look back to their rearward movement, but strike them in the middle. Even though they are numerous they can be taken. The Tao for attacking the arrogant is not to not engage their advance front."

—**Sun Tzu, author,** *The Art of War*

PART THREE

The Way Forward for America

"It ain't over till the fat lady sings."
Traditional American Expression

12 Harden All Targets

We learned a lesson from President George H.W. Bush's Structural Impediments Initiative in the late 1980s. These talks were aimed at reducing the American trade deficit with Japan. The American argument was that it was not tariffs that discouraged Japanese from buying more American products. It was the *keiretsu* system in which large companies were linked with each other and with smaller companies through stock-holdings and other long-term relationships. They controlled the distribution channels for goods, which made it more difficult for the Americans to break in.

The talks never succeeded because the U.S. government was asking the Japanese to give up the heart of their economic model. And it had considerable clout. We wrote the Japanese constitution after World War II and still had 50,000 American soldiers stationed there. We had twice as large a population, including a larger market. And the country depended on the United States for protection from both China and North Korea. But the Japanese never budged on the structural impediments. It was just how their economy worked. We were trying to change how they organized themselves as a people.

We have far less clout today with China. We don't have any military forces on their soil and they have a population more than four times larger than ours. We had no involvement in developing their form of government. There is no chance that China is going to give up on its technology ambitions because it regards the acquisition and development of key technologies as essential to its rise to power. Technology power is commercial power is national power. Backing down would be a humiliation for President Xi.

The American government has not yet faced up to this central reality. President Trump's negotiators seem to believe that tariffs will force the Chinese government to change its technological course, that somehow it will "fold" under the pressure. But if you understand the history, you know the Chinese party-state will not back down and cannot. China's bid for technology is non-negotiable. If the government were to back down, it would allow the Chinese nation to be subjected to the same policy of "containment" that the United States used against the Soviet Union.

Thus, the hacking is going to continue and the economic espionage is going to continue, as well as the other patterns of involvement in the fabric of American life. The patterns may shift but will not be voluntarily halted. Xi may agree to delay some elements of his Made in China 2025 plan and ease some pressures on U.S. companies. He may agree to purchase more American goods. But the Chinese government's fundamental goals will remain in place as long as Xi is in power, which could easily mean five or 10 years or longer. "The attempts to acquire foreign technology will continue, though the methods will shift," Derek Scissors, the resident China expert at the American Enterprise Institute in Washington told me.

If the China government's deep game cannot be negotiated away, the burden of adjustment falls on us. There has been a spectacular void in the commentary on what the United States must do to confront China's ambitions inside our country.

The first step in a national response to China's intrusions and espionage is hardening our targets. We need to play better defense. Some experts in law enforcement believe in "naming and shaming" China's hackers, but that reflects a Western view of morality. It suggests that the hackers will feel shame and therefore alter their behavior. But the Chinese don't share that moral platform. If a Chinese individual or agency is publicly identified as having hacked an American target, that person or that agency might be quietly shifted somewhere else to continue their work, hopefully without getting caught the next time. They are not impressed by "Wanted by the FBI" posters. Another reason the hacking will continue is that it is remarkably cheap compared to the billions of dollars of gain that it offers. It is essentially risk-free.

In response, the Department of Justice and the FBI need to redouble their efforts and the FBI needs to make sure that Joey Chun's betrayal has not left any trap doors behind. A number of important federal IT infrastructure efforts are underway. The Department of Homeland Security is attempting to establish itself as the key clearing house for information about cyber threats, as specified by the Cybersecurity and Infrastructure Security Agency Act of 2018.[1] The U.S. Strategic Command is building a new command and control facility in Nebraska[2]. The Pentagon is about to choose a vendor to build a $10 billion, ten-year cloud computing project called the Joint Enterprise Defense Infrastructure, or JEDI.[3] Everyone involved in building and protecting the government's IT infrastructure should assume that Chinese government-affiliated hackers will come knocking on the door—if they are not already inside.

For its part, the Pentagon needs to move faster to eliminate the hundreds of defects in its IT system identified by its own inspector general. It needs to better protect not only its communications networks with major defense suppliers but to extend that aegis of protection to small and mid-sized defense contractors. It also needs to improve efforts to protect its weapons systems from hacking, which a report by the

General Accountability Office (GAO) said are badly needed.[4] GAO investors said that using relatively simple tools and techniques, they were able to take control of the systems in major weapons without being detected. It's possible that the U.S. Navy's systems have been riddled with hacks and there is a particular urgency for it to reclaim control of its systems and networks. As usual, the generals and admirals are ready for the last war, not the next one.

Moreover, the Pentagon needs to make sure that its existing computers have not been infected by the chip that the People's Liberation Army had installed on the motherboards of servers purchased by different arms of the military, as *BusinessWeek* described. And the military also needs to rededicate itself anew to understanding its supply chain vulnerabilities because if a supply chain runs through China, there is a risk of compromise. There are signs that the Pentagon has started pivoting from the war on terror to the competition with China and to a lesser extent a much weaker Russia. The Pentagon said as much in a 2017 report describing future threats. But it is behind the curve. The Chinese have been preparing for this day for years.

It could take years to fully safeguard all the government's computer systems, if it is indeed possible. So many have been penetrated and we know that Chinese government-backed hackers can hide for years in a system and "hop" into other systems when the time is right. "I wouldn't describe the government as wide open, but obviously it is not closed either," Grotto, the former NSC cyber expert, told me. "Perfect security is never possible unless we stop using computers, which is not viable. Assessing cyber threats is always an exercise in risk management, which means accepting some degree of risk. What we can hope for is to make it as costly as possible for any adversary to break in and then get really good at hunting for adversary activity on the network and be able to continue to operate despite being penetrated. In other words, we need to develop resilience in the face of known compromise."

He likened fighting cyber intrusions to coping with hurricanes. "You can't defend against a hurricane," he said. "The best you can do is fortify your systems and develop strategies for resilience and then recovery."

One major vulnerability, which hints at the scale of the challenge, is that nearly all federal agencies manage their own email systems. "Email is a huge issue," Grotto said. "Surveys that cyber security companies have done on success rates for phishing in organizations have shown that it's almost inevitable that an adversary will persuade someone inside the organization to click on a link or open a malicious file." One initiative he helped start during the Obama administration, which the Trump administration is still pursuing, was to gradually persuade agencies to shift to a fewer number of email systems that could be better protected and operated more cheaply. "Rather than having every agency do its own email, for commodity services like that, we should find a much smaller number of providers who offer that service to other agencies," he said. That would reduce the government's "attack surface."

* * *

It's absolutely essential that we keep Huawei and ZTE out of our telecommunications systems and those of our allies as we move toward the next level of speed, the so-called 5G technology. AT&T and Verizon, and others, are spending billions to make this next leap to higher computing speeds, starting in 2019. Even if Huawei and ZTE argue that they can do it more cheaply, the odds are overwhelming that they would build in trap doors or other ways to access our networks. I once regarded that suspicion as pure paranoia. But now after conducting the research for this book, I think it's very real, and other informed people agree. In a report in November 2018, the U.S.-China Economic and Security Review Commission warned that China's position as the world's largest manufacturer of Internet-connected devices created "numerous points of vulnerability for intelligence collection, cyberattacks, industrial control, or censorship."[5]

There's no question that Huawei or ZTE would accommodate a request by the Chinese government for access to their networks. "Because China has an authoritarian government that believes the Communist Party should control everything, and everything in the country should serve the interests of the party, it is nearly unimaginable that any Chinese company can say no to government requests, especially if they are made repeatedly and in the name of national security," technology columnist Li Yuan wrote in *The New York Times*.[6]

Because AT&T and Verizon depend on foreign manufacturers for much of their gear, one idea, broached by Mancini, the former Homeland Security official, is to implement a system of third-party accreditation, such as what Underwriter's Laboratory (UL) does for electric appliances and light bulbs. Such a third party could inspect and test telecom equipment made abroad to certify that it does not contain backdoors or vulnerabilities. Germany's cybersecurity watchdog said in December that it would set up security labs to do just that.[7]

* * *

On other fronts, Senators Marco Rubio, a Republican from Florida, and Mark R. Warner, a Virginia Democrat, in January 2019 introduced a bill that would create an Office of Critical Technologies and Security at the White House level in response to Chinese government intrusions on U.S. networks and assaults on U.S. technology targets.[8] It would aim to improve cooperation among federal agencies and develop a long-term strategy against theft of intellectual property and risks to supply chains. "China continues to conduct a coordinated assault on U.S. intellectual property, U.S. businesses, and our government networks and information with the full backing of the Chinese Communist Party," said Rubio, who has been one of the most consistent critics of China's actions in the United States. "The United States needs a more coordinated approach to directly counter this critical threat and ensure we better protect U.S. technology." That's a good first step, but the office, as proposed, seems to concentrate mostly on defense. It needs to do more, as I will outline in the next chapter.

As evidenced by the introduction of the Rubio-Warner bill, the strengthening of CFIUS and export control rules, the passage of a cybersecurity law, and the continued indictments of bad Chinese cyber actors, there are signs that the U.S. government is waking up to the pattern of Chinese government actions inside the United States. The proverbial alarm bells are ringing. But ultimately, the federal government is going to have to become much more sophisticated—and quickly—if it wants to address the full scale of China's technology acquisition efforts. "The problem is that we don't yet understand what technology we need to know more about," said one well-placed source in Washington who requested anonymity because she has strong views and was not authorized to speak. "The experts in the government don't yet understand how technology is transferred, whether it's through venture capital investing or other vectors.

"When it comes to AI, what are we trying to protect?" she continued. "Is it the data that is being used or is it the logic (the algorithms) or is it the final product? What's the most important thing to think about protecting or monitoring when it's being transferred to another country?" The Commerce Department, for example, is just beginning to identify key emerging technologies that should be subject to export controls, as mandated by the 2019 defense appropriations bill.

"We know that technology theft will happen in one form or another," she went on. "The question is what level of friction can we add to the process of theft? Right now, we do a pretty poor job as a government advising start-up companies and others on what the nature of the threat is, whether it is cyber theft or industrial espionage. We should be very clear about the nature of the threat so that companies can take this seriously and institute new cyber policies and have a better sense of what their employees are doing or when their network is under attack. It's providing an honest assessment of what's really happening, which we don't really do right now."

She said the U.S. government is "a little behind" in understanding emerging technologies. "What is happening in bioinformatics, in artificial intelligence, in machine learning?" she asked. "It's hard to develop any rules or regulations around a technology if you don't understand what's really happening. Does it become obsolete in six months or a year? How do you create a dynamic list of critical technologies? How do you make sure you are consulting widely with academia, the private sector and other parts of government? These are things we don't do right now. We have a process of notice and comment and requests for information. These are systems based on a legacy of how technology was developed back in the day when you were just worried about final products. There has to be a concerted effort to bring in relevant stakeholders so that they can opine on what is actually happening in technology and what's important and not important."

The gap between government and the tech sector was particularly clear when Facebook's Mark Zuckerberg testified before Congress and committee members asked him rudimentary questions. Congressmen who are supposed to be the nation's policy makers lacked basic knowledge about how Facebook operates. "There is a fundamental mismatch between what is happening in the technology companies and what our policy makers know," she concluded. Obviously, that gap has to be dramatically narrowed if the United States is going to protect itself against Chinese technology grabs.

* * *

The private sector has an even bigger challenge than government, as reflected in how easily the APT10 hacking group penetrated the nation's cloud computing system over a period of years. "Most victims of cyberattacks are in the private sector; the most relevant attacks on critical infrastructure and political health happen in this space rather than against classified government networks," FireEye's Porter wrote.[9]

Companies of all sizes have to recognize that they need intrusion detection systems and skilled operators who can detect intrusions and repel the attackers. The private sector should be working more aggressively with federal agencies to share information about what "threat vectors" America's intelligence agencies have detected. "Current practice takes months or years to declassify useful information about cyber threats and share it, but since the front line in this battle is

the private sector, that approach doesn't make a lot of sense,"
Porter told me. The speed at which information is shared
should improve now that the Department of Homeland
Security has been given wider powers, as specified by the
cybersecurity law enacted in 2018.

It's not good enough to do the work of hardening
targets only within a single company because, increasingly,
companies are linking themselves electronically to each other
to speed the flow of information about what customers want
and what the supply chain needs to manufacture to satisfy
those demands. Companies must recognize that their entire IT
ecosystem of suppliers and customers must be secured, which
will be difficult because companies have been globalizing their
supply chains for decades in pursuit of greater efficiencies.

Companies have long worried about the resiliency of
their supply chains in the event of natural disruptions like
floods or hurricanes. It is only now that they are beginning to
recognize the security risk. "Corporate supply chains are
growing targets of foreign intelligence entities," the National
Counterintelligence and Security Center, located within the
office of the Director of National Intelligence, warned in
January 2019 as it launched an effort to help the private sector
respond to cyber threats.[iii] "Adversaries are bypassing hardened
corporate defenses by using less-secure suppliers and vendors
as surreptitious entry points to surveil, sabotage, and steal
information from companies' networks."

The challenges will be magnified as industry pushes
toward the Internet of Things, when billions of sensors,
cameras and other devices will be connected. Access to any
single device could lead to access of many others.

Some business sectors have taken cyber threats more
seriously than others. "The financial services sector, particularly
the big players, has really put a lot of capital into this," Grotto,

the former NSC expert, told me. "The big telecommunications and Internet service providers are very good and very sophisticated."

But after that, there is a steep fall-off in the private sector's preparedness. "The electricity sector is waking up to this but they are for the most part regulated monopolies," Grotto explained. "They have public utility commissions and other stakeholders they have to manage to build more budget space for security."

Why is it, if massive Chinese party-state cyber attacks are occurring and making headlines, that there does not seem to be a more urgent response? "There is a lot of alarm," Grotto said. "Most of the critical infrastructure is owned and operated by the private sector. What's the appropriate mix of incentives and disincentives to get companies to do the right things when it comes to managing the cyber risks? How do we even know what the right thing is when it comes to measuring return on investment?"

At the end of the day, it seems that American consumers are not sufficiently outraged by the leaking of their personal data that they are demanding that businesses do a better job of protecting it. "The demand signal for more security is still pretty weak across the board, for consumers and from businesses," Grotto said. "Until that demand signal is stronger, the prevailing practice will be to under-invest in cyber security."

* * *

When it comes to human penetration, the GE case that resulted in the arrest of the MSS's Xu was a hopeful sign that more companies will work with federal authorities when they identify a potential problem. At least some companies have been reluctant to seek federal help because they fear possible publicity and damage to their share prices. "What I think is important," Campbell, the 25-year FBI veteran, said, "is that the FBI, the Department of Homeland Security, the Commerce Department and other agencies have been engaged in significant and organized outreach to universities, the defense industrial base, other companies with sensitive technologies, the national laboratory system, and other R&D entities to help them identify where they may be vulnerable to information that would be desired by the Chinese and other adversaries."

They also have tried to communicate what to look for regarding individuals within their institutions who could potentially present a threat and implement insider threat programs. "That initiative is not perfect," Campbell acknowledged. "It is not going to stop every threat."

That means managements of companies possessing technologies targeted by the Chinese government must devise ways to conduct security checks of all employees. Managements of companies that possess sensitive technologies could require all employees to fill out standardized forms once a year, as the FBI does for its personnel with Top Secret clearances, to list their foreign trips and to list any representatives of foreign governments they may have met. That would start creating a paper trail and could ultimately trip up anyone engaged in espionage. Having all employees at key companies fill out the forms seems to be the only way we can remain true to our commitment to non-discrimination while at the same time possibly detecting breeches.

Campbell wrestled with this tough issue while at the FBI. "That's an area that's near and dear to me," he told me. "When I was in the FBI, one of my roles was leading civil rights investigations and protecting civil liberties. When I was in the bureau, we didn't seek to target a particular people, a race or an ethnicity. We were identifying and targeting threats. That's what our strategies were based on. As a result, whatever individuals might present those threats, based on legitimate information and intelligence and evidence, those are what the FBI and the Department of Justice would build their case on. It would not be appropriate to identify who are the Chinese nationals or those with Chinese background and then target them. What companies should look at there is their vulnerabilities by conducting a risk assessment. The FBI can help them craft those strategies to make sure that they are threat-based and not targeting specific individuals because of their backgrounds or beliefs or anything like that."

I was able to persuade one major company to share its thinking about these issues strictly on background. "We treat all our employees equally, and we don't single out Chinese employees for any special screening or procedures," the company said. "All our employees are subject to rigorous training programs to teach them how to conduct themselves legally and ethically, and how to avoid potential pitfalls that could compromise our intellectual property. And our hiring processes involve both internal and external sources and we continuously evaluate ways to strengthen and update our systems with respect to our data and our hiring practices in light of the full range of emerging threats."

In other words, it can be done—IP can be protected without discriminating against Chinese employees. It requires training, better hiring practices and monitoring. All the work of safeguarding America's systems and protecting their integrity against espionage is expensive, and might cut into quarterly profits, but it is necessary. It has to become a national priority.

* * *

On another front, we need to rethink our scientific community's approach to conducting completely open research, as demonstrated by the manipulation by Chinese students and professors of the National Institutes of Health peer review process. Universities could do a better job of enforcing the requirement that researchers who receive NIH grants also disclose any other sources of funding and other disclosure requirements could be tightened, but either of those strategies depend on the willingness of a researcher to tell the truth, which has been conspicuously lacking. The FBI is seeking to work with universities to control the problem and has even circulated a guide to "academic espionage tradecraft." But those solutions do not address the fundamental problem.

The only logical course is to gradually reduce the presence of Chinese students and researchers in the inner sanctums of our cutting-edge research facilities. Some of the Chinese-born students may belong in those research facilities, where they are making genuine contributions. Others may not belong. We need to figure out how to tell the difference and have that knowledge inform our hiring decisions.

Screening Chinese applicants to American universities on the basis of their social media posts, as some in the administration have proposed, is pointless and would require enormous resources to achieve. The key pressure point is what happens after a student graduates and goes to work in a government laboratory or is hired by an American technology company. The Trump administration in mid-2018 did quietly take some actions affecting Chinese students. The steps were never clearly spelled out in public but they seemed to limit Chinese students in fields such as robotics and advanced manufacturing to one-year visas after they graduate rather than five years.[10] The government and universities may need to take further, similar steps.

13 Toward a Winning Technology Strategy

When Americans can agree on the need to respond to a challenge, our institutions can cooperate and collaborate in tremendously effective ways. It's time to do that once again. If the Chinese have established an industrial policy to dominate certain industries, and are either misappropriating American technology or buying it on the cheap, we need to craft an American response or a series of responses.

We need the kind of resolve that led business, education and government to come together to develop the atomic bomb and end World War II. We displayed similar urgency and cooperation after the Soviets surprised us with the success of their Sputnik satellite launch in the 1950s. That spurred us to create our own highly successful space program with President John F. Kennedy, in 1961, setting a goal of putting a man on the moon within a decade. It happened just eight years later.

Likewise, President Nixon launched the war on cancer in 1971, which resulted in an explosion of research and development that has given the United States leadership in biotechnology and genomics. It was also collaboration between the military, government and universities that gave birth to the Internet. The Republican administration of President Bush helped save the American semiconductor industry from Japanese competitive pressures by creating a government-business-education consortium called Sematech and it helped save the American auto industry by starting the process of creating a North American Free Trade Agreement (NAFTA), which President Clinton signed into law. That gave American carmakers a continental-scale platform to drive down their costs. "Everybody saw Sputnik," Dave Vieau, the former CEO of A123 Systems, told me. "But nobody sees the China challenge. We have met the enemy and the enemy is us. We have not mobilized our resources." He did business with Chinese entities for 23 years and was involved in technology and manufacturing for his entire career.

On other fronts, we are deliberately moving slowly at the moment on AI and genetic editing because we have ethical debates about these technologies. Employees of Google have protested against the company offering its technology to the U.S. military even while the company is said to be working on a search engine for the Chinese market that complies with the edicts of Chinese censors.

But the Chinese party-state is not having any hesitations. It is plunging forward with facial recognition technology, as well as AI. We must create our own agreements on what we regard as ethical and humane, and what isn't. Then we need to get on with advancing the technologies. Congress in December 2018 approved a bill aimed at speeding American development of quantum computing, an area of key Chinese interest and one that could transform the world of computers and telecommunications. The legislation somehow avoided the usual political firestorms and was signed into law. It provides $1.2 billion into the quantum research budgets of the Energy Department, the National Institute of Standards and Technology, NASA and the National Science Foundation.[1] Trump also issued an executive order promoting AI research. Those were positive steps, but decidedly modest in comparison with China's ambitious and well-funded research programs.

We need to establish a mechanism for coordinating American actions on critical technologies. This is an old debate dating back to the days of the Japanese challenge. But now it has become more urgent because of the sheer scale and ambition of the Chinese government's efforts. Let's call it the Office of Strategic Technologies. Strengthening CFIUS to defend American companies against controlling investments of acquisitions is only half the battle.

The other half of the battle is to work with American companies to identify technology road maps and make sure the companies with the best ideas have access to the capital markets. The collection of information about all the players and all the competing ideas in a particular technology that is identified as being strategic would be an essential function of this office. The Pentagon and intelligence agencies have a stake in this, as does the White House Office of Science and Technology Policy (OSTP) and the Department of Energy. It should be at the White House level. The OSTP could make up the heart of the new Office of Strategic Technologies because it already has attempted to play part of that role during previous administrations.

This idea is very similar to the bill that Rubio and Warner introduced, but their legislation is aimed primarily at playing defense. As they envision the office, it would not place an emphasis on nurturing new American technologies. They also are proposing a brand new agency. I argue that if we are trying to streamline the federal government, it would be better to use the existing OSTP as the heart of the effort.

I debated these ideas with Kennedy. "I am always worried about new organizational changes," he said. "I think the Office of Science and Technology Policy, if it were staffed with the right people and given the right mission, could play the role you want this new office to play. The proliferation of new offices usually creates more problems than benefits, often resulting in no improvement in the state of the nation's economy or our national security."

The Obama Administration used the OSTP as a key policy-making tool, but Trump has not placed a priority on science. In fact, he's done precisely the opposite, particularly in the environmental sphere. So the OSTP has been allowed to atrophy from a staff of about 300 to roughly 100 today, Kennedy estimates. And it was not until January 2019 that the office was given a chief, as opposed to an acting chief. The Senate confirmed Kelvin Droegemeier, a meteorologist from Norman, Okla., who was once was vice president for research at the University of Oklahoma.[2] He also served as vice chair of the National Science Board. U.S. academic leaders are said to be eager to work with him, but his profile does not suggest he would be comfortable in the AI laboratories in Palo Alto or the biotech labs of Cambridge. Ironically, Droegemeier was delayed in assuming his new position by the partial government shut-down and winter weather. The ability of the OSTP to fulfill a larger role is "a huge question mark," Kennedy said.

Clearly, these are complex organizational issues. Whatever bureaucratic formulation prevails, we need a leading technology policy body that both protects and promotes the best ideas. The office should be multi-disciplinary, meaning it should include people with business experience as well as academics with deep expertise in a particular field. Moreover, the culture of collaboration among federal agencies involved in protecting and advancing technologies needs to be enhanced. The linkages should be tighter.

We also should learn from the mistakes made in the financial failure of A123 Systems, the lithium-ion battery company that was at the forefront of building a new industry with thousands of jobs but was ultimately purchased by a Chinese state-affiliated company. Government funding at the federal level is always going to be subjected to political crossfire. It's much the same at the gubernatorial and mayoral level. A newly elected candidate always seems to criticize funding or incentives granted to large companies by his or her predecessor.

Vieau, the former CEO, argues that the government should work with existing clusters of technology companies to declare one area as a "center of global excellence" for a particular technology. That means there would be one center of global excellence for biotechnology, say, perhaps the San Francisco Bay area. But that would anger the other biotechnology clusters in San Diego and Boston/Cambridge.

I think it is more realistic to declare each cluster to be a center of excellence and to attempt to help them grow organically and out-innovate everyone else in the world, including the Chinese. The Office of Strategic Technologies would, for example, declare Pittsburgh as a global center of robotics and autonomous driving because of Carnegie Mellon University's leading role in that field and summon all U.S. players in robotics to attend at least one industry-specific meeting. Upstate New York in the Albany area could be a center of nanotechnology and thus a rallying point for the entire industry. San Diego is the capital of wireless communications because of the role of Qualcomm, which is based there. The strategic technologies office could start with one or two critical technologies and gradually build to accommodate others depending on their levels of need. The semiconductor industry already has Sematech and is dominant over China. It may not need help as urgently as other sectors.

Whatever policy decision is made, the symbolism of recognizing these clusters and arguing that they should be excellent on a global basis would be powerful. "We need to do something like Nixon did with cancer," Vieau says. "The core identification of a category that we are committed to is half the battle. We all know the arguments against it: Nobody wants to pick a winner. Nobody wants to make a decision. But I think there would be congressional support for centers of excellence around the country."

This strategy might avoid the dilemma of picking a certain company as the winner of government largesse. If a sector were identified as strategic to our future, the office could seek to promote the health of the whole ecosystem, not just a single politically connected player. We usually don't accept government-controlled efforts but we have the flexibility and pragmatism to assemble the key players in a room and agree upon a strategy for a specific technology.

In short, we need to boost the ecosystems of our leading technology clusters, which I have been following since editing and co-writing a 1992 *BusinessWeek* cover story entitled "Hot Spots."[3] We published that piece well before Harvard's Michael Porter starting using the term "clusters" to describe these complex ecosystems that have spawned so much of America's growth since then.[4] We can continue to improve how these clusters work—and create new ones. We should boost R&D funding for universities to create more advances in key areas and then license the technology to entrepreneurs. Other government funding could help key universities improve the pay packages for professors and graduate students to give them incentive to invent and commercialize. Overall, federal research and development spending increased 12.8 percent in 2018 to $176.8 billion, a positive sign, according to the American Association for the Advancement of Science.[5] But federal government spending on R&D should be increased even further.

Universities should be encouraged to open up the valves and accelerate the transfer of technologies developed in their labs into the hands of the private sector. Right now, many technology transfer departments at universities are playing a game of defense, trying to prevent good ideas from being commercialized without sufficient benefit to the university. The classic case was how Gatorade emerged from the University of Florida's athletic program and became a commercial success without the university gaining from it. On another front, state and local governments could increase the tax benefits they are currently offering to companies that start out with a new idea from a university or a Department of Energy laboratory.

The idea is to stimulate many cities' and regions' competitive juices. "You get momentum behind a certain technology," Vieau argues. "The students, the community, everybody knows what we're doing as opposed to having it be random."

The strategic technology office would have the power to convene all the key players in a particular technological field and ask, What is working? What is not? If university leaders, angel investors, venture capitalists, start-ups and large companies, chambers of commerce, economic development officials and other stakeholders were to sit down and discuss how to cooperate more robustly in developing a technology, that could be powerful. The government would not dictate the future. It would create platforms that allow the private sector and other players in regional ecosystems to do what they do best.

This office should have access to an investment fund, but it should never seek to be the dominant funder of any company or any technology. A modest sum of $500 million to $1 billion could be impactful. It would be authorized to make small, non-controlling investments in either emerging technologies with promise or in larger, more mature companies which have promising ideas but have hit financial difficulty.

This was perhaps one of the mistakes that the Obama Administration made in trying to create a solar power industry and an electric car industry—its funding was too dominant and hence the recipients did not respond to market signals.

If the Office of Strategic Technologies built tight linkages with the Pentagon's DARPA and other military offices seeking to tap into emerging technologies, and if it built similar linkages to the CIA's venture capital arm called In-Q-Tel and the Department of Energy's national weapons laboratories and its ARPA-E investment arm, that might set the stage for venture capitalists in the private sector to gain confidence in a particular technology, thereby easing the shortage of capital that causes so many technology companies to turn to Chinese money or fail to develop. The Pentagon's Defense Innovation Unit has won approval to set up a new venture capital arm like the CIA's and is seeking funding for it. That would add a new player to the team. Each of these entities could put up what insiders are calling "stimulus capital."

The new strategic technology office also might be able to encourage more capital to flow to sectors that venture capitalists have not paid as much attention to. Their money has overwhelmingly flowed into the hands of Internet-affiliated software start-ups, because of the expectation that they will reach profitability relatively quickly and not require large capital investments. But robotics makers in Pittsburgh or advanced energy researchers in Ohio have a much more difficult time obtaining VC funding.

Enlisting private investors to help the office achieve its objectives is incredibly important. The legislation creating the office could specify that the office has the power to designate certain industries as "critical" or "strategic." Then private sector investors who support companies in those industries would enjoy lower tax rates or accelerated depreciation for a finite period of time, say, five years. The legislation would have to be crafted carefully because the World Trade Organization has very specific rules about government's subsidizing industry. But it can be done.

The strategic technologies office also could broker deal-making. If it learns about a company with a promising technology that is having financial difficulty, it could make an introduction to other richer companies that might have an interest in a merger or acquisition. Perhaps the office could make a symbolic investment in such a transaction to give an acquirer additional confidence.

"Ultimately, we have a better engine for (technology) development than the Chinese do," argues Vieau. We just need to rev up the engine.

* * *

One example where an integrated inter-departmental approach could be effective is in rare earths, the metals few civilians have ever heard of, but which play a crucial role in all types of technology manufacturing, including military goods. Scandium, for example, is used in aerospace components, yitrium is used in televisions, and lanthanum is used in battery electrodes and camera lenses. There are 17 of these rare earths and the U.S. depends on imports to meet about half its demand. China, meanwhile, possesses 90 percent of the world's supplies, which obviously puts American companies at a steep disadvantage in the event of disruption. Rare earths could one day emerge as a crucial choke-point for the Pentagon in its efforts to obtain the weapons and other materiel it needs.

One Chicago-based entrepreneur, James Litinsky, has purchased the Mountain Pass mine in California out of bankruptcy[6]. It is the only U.S.-based provider of rare earths.

He and his investment group have spent about $200 million so far. But he has to send his rare earths to China, which has lower environmental standards, for processing. China has an infrastructure of processors, refiners and parts-makers that make rare earths actually usable. Rare earths like Litinsky's are first turned into alloys and then into magnets.

So far, it's not clear whether Litinsky will be able to build the processing capabilities he needs in the United States and even whether he can stay in business. The Office of Strategy Technologies could engineer a plan to make sure the United States develops the full range of rare earth capabilities on U.S. soil. The Department of Energy has experts who make nuclear weapons and know how to handle dangerous metals. The CIA, Defense Department, NASA and the Energy Department all have vested interests in rare earths. Surely, a support package could be put in place involving loans, investments and perhaps outright grants. Each agency could put up, say, $10 million in stimulus capital. Other private sector investors would be encouraged to take part. The United States could fill an obvious hole in its strategic security by helping a private sector company survive. (I would make an exception in this case, arguing that the federal government could help a single company. It is such an important sector and the United States has only one player in it. In effect, the company is the industry.)

As of the moment, there are many officials in the government, particularly in the Defense Department, who want to help Litinsky, but they feel their hands are tied—even though The White House issued an Executive Order in December 2017 urging all agencies to accelerate support for rare earths. "The government is already motivated enough," Litinsky told me. "The Department of Defense wants to help us. Others want to help us. You go around the government and people say, 'What you're doing is great, but what is our power to help you?' You have to come up with a specific law or authorization they have that allows them to help you. Without a tangible tool for them, they usually only provide a sympathetic ear and sometimes introductions to other people across government. But so far, nothing has happened as a result of the Executive Order. We have not gotten any tangible assistance."

A self-sufficient supply chain beginning with rare earths all the way to the point of making magnets and actual products is crucial for several of the military's priorities. "We need rare earths for national security whether for space technology or electric vehicles," Litinsky said. "Another big area is the future of Navy weaponry. A lot of its guns use electronic pulses that require big magnets. Some very sophisticated drones also use a lot of magnets. If you think about the future of trains, or the future of any advanced electric infrastructure, these things are likely going to require rare earth materials."

Litinsky is a big believer in the notion that the office of strategic technologies could be empowered to declare certain industries to be national priorities and that investors would therefore receive special tax treatment or other incentives. "At the end of the day, to build any industry from scratch requires a lot of capital," he said. "You need the private markets. The government is not going to directly invest over $5 billion in this or, if they did, it would still require industrial expertise and years of execution. By changing the cost of capital, you might get accelerated action by private industry."

He also thinks that American buyers of rare earth products ought to give his products a preference. "Why is it that Apple and Tesla get away with saying they are doing great things for the world when they are buying materials from the

Congo and from China that were made in ways that are not environmentally friendly?" he asked. "One reason Mountain Pass went into bankruptcy is that they spent so much money building a state-of-the-art, environmentally friendly facility. We have a dry tailings process, which is extremely rare in mining. It's one of the cleanest mining chemical processes in the world. That means we start with the burden of having a very high operating cost for that piece of the process relative to the global competition. Our ore body is the best in the world so our mission is to make sure that we are efficient enough to be a low-cost producer globally anyway. However, shouldn't American industry be accountable for their entire supply chains? They should be willing to pay a premium for the environmental advantage of our materials. Some of what we need is from the government, but we also need industry support. It needs to be holistic."

"Holistic" is the key word. "If you look at the Chinese system as opposed to the American system, in the Chinese approach, the state and the family are one," Litinsky said. "The state acts like a family. The American approach is very individualistic. For America, one of the things we need to learn if we are going to compete in this new world where China is a hegemonic power, we also need to take on some characteristics and recognize that we are a family, so to speak. I think Mountain Pass is a great opportunity for my investors. But I also believe this is extremely critical infrastructure for the future of our country and the future of democracy."

* * *

This proposal for a broad technology policy inevitably re-opens the old argument about "industrial policy," a politically charged term. In previous fights over this subject, opponents of government involvement in promoting new technologies have argued that government should not be involved in "picking winners and losers." That was the subtext for the bitter political fight over Solyndra, the California-based solar company.

What these opponents have not recognized, at least not publically, is that the U.S. government has had a huge impact in identifying and promoting new technologies, such as the Internet, autonomous driving (DARPA was a driving force in launching that industry) and GPS satellite positioning. The National Institutes of Health have spawned the biotech and genomics industries. The National Science Foundation has also spent billions supporting R&D. The Department of Energy's national weapons labs such as Argonne and Sandia are treasure chests of advanced technology, only a small portion of which is commercialized.

In a previous era, we could afford to allow this argument over "industrial policy" to tie our decision-making in knots because, in part, the Japanese competitive challenge did not prove to be as powerful as it appeared to be in the late 1980s. The creation of Sematech and NAFTA also helped American companies defend themselves. But perhaps the biggest factor is that the Japanese challenge was eclipsed by a much bigger challenge emanating from China, a country with more than 10 times the population.

Now that the government of a fifth of humankind is making a conscious, centralized assault on American technologies, on U.S. soil, it seems only logical that we should reorganize our agencies so that we have a clear focus on strategic technologies and making sure that American companies have viable roles in them.

But we are confused, as Kennedy of the CSIS explained. "I'm not sure if this is so much an organizational problem as it is an ideological one," he told me. "The U.S. certainly does in some respect have difficulties thinking strategically about different industries, about different countries and challenges to U.S. global leadership. The U.S. is allergic to industrial policy. We have such a strong commitment to the free market, which has resulted in a very efficient economy but there are occasionally market failures that don't get addressed. Some of these technologies should be viewed as public goods and the support for them should be strengthened."

A case in point is the push for all-electric cars. China's government is spending billions to build a complete infrastructure of parts, a supply chain, manufacturing, consumer demand, infrastructure and other elements involved in establishing a new industry. "China's electric car industry is developing quite rapidly," said Kennedy, who has spent 30 years studying China's development efforts. "The Chinese government has put an amazing amount of resources into both production of electric cars and demand for them. It has supported the entire supply chain from the raw materials that go into batteries to all the different components in an electric car to the final assemblers."

The United States has some excellent researchers in the field of electric cars, including batteries and energy storage. They have received funding from the Department of Energy's ARPA-E arm and other sources. "But the electric car market in the U.S. is puny," Kennedy continued. "If you are an inventor in this sector, once you're done receiving ARPA-E funding or other federal government funding, and you achieve a breakthrough, you want to commercialize that breakthrough. But there is almost no place in the United States to do so. So scientists and engineers get up and take that technology to China. It totally makes sense when they do their commercial calculus. China has a big market that is moving forward and the United States does not."

The United States could try to prevent scientists and engineers from taking promising technologies to China. "But at the end of the day, the best way to protect innovators in energy storage and batteries is developing a market in the United States for these technologies," Kennedy argued.

Some states such as California, where Tesla is headquartered, are trying to promote the development of electric cars. Of course, the Trump Administration is moving away from helping establish an electric car industry, by reducing the federal tax credit for buyers of electric vehicles from \$7,000 to \$3,500, as of Jan. 1. Tesla is resorting to lay-offs to lower its costs so that it can price the Model 3 in a way that will attract more buyers.[7] Any action to help an electric car industry establish itself will have to await a new administration. But in theory, Kennedy said the federal government should work with state governments to encourage consumer demand and to build the infrastructure of charging stations that would ease the issue of "range anxiety," or running out of juice.

So it's time for the United States to break out of its ideological logjam when it comes to developing key industries. Not every industry of the future needs help, but some clearly do. And it's ludicrous to assume that the same governmental structure that's been in place since the 1950s can be effective in the face of China's penetration of American companies and their R&D labs. It is a new era and that demands stronger, more effective government. We must create more cohesion in our institutional structures. That's not un-American. It's called common sense.

14 Upskilling and Reshoring

Having a successful technology strategy probably will not work unless we recognize that we need to do a better job of bringing along those Americans and those regions who have fallen behind in a globalized, technology-intensive world. Millions of Americans—particularly those with college degrees, travel experience, exposure to different languages, and technological proficiency—have raced ahead. For years, American leaders assumed that displaced workers or others left behind would catch up—but they haven't. As a result, we have hard core pockets of poverty, drug use and unemployment in both urban and rural settings.

We have not created a consistent and clear national educational infrastructure for training and re-training. Many of the displaced have accepted a vision promoted by the current administration that the clock can be turned back and that old jobs can be magically revived. That is false. The only way forward is to embrace the future. I've argued for years that we need to revive our vocational and technical schools, including community colleges to help get that done. It's incredibly ironic that millions of Americans have dropped out of the work force at the same time that employers report they cannot fill 7.1 million job openings.[1]

We do a great job producing Ph.D's, MBA's and MD.s, but we have failed to create enough welders, machinists, quality engineers and production technicians. Many American high schools eliminated their shop classes years ago as manufacturing moved out of the country. If we want new technology companies to grow into billion-dollar companies with thousands of employees, we need to recognize that the lack of skills is perhaps the single biggest factor limiting that growth.

Successful models do exist. One is in upstate New York. The State of New York, led by Governor Andrew Cuomo, launched an effort to create a nanotechnology and semiconductor industry there, which has consistently ranked as one of the hardest-hit economic areas in the country. At first, it seemed like Mission Impossible. Why would any semiconductor maker in its right mind locate a facility in an economically distressed region?

The county of Saratoga, which includes the university town of Saratoga Springs, smelled opportunity and started building industry-academic partnerships to start training students in all aspects of making semiconductors. It's an old chicken-and-the egg riddle—do you train people to attract manufacturing or do you obtain a plant and then start training people? No manufacturer had yet committed to locating there, but the Saratoga County Prosperty Partnership, an economic development coalition, started working with state universities and community colleges. One program was developed by the State University of New York's Hudson Valley Community College called the Training and Education Center for Semiconductor Manufacturing and Alternative and Renewable Technologies (TEC-SMART.) It was located in the town of Malta. Several other state and local initiatives were launched to create the right skills sets.[2]

Against all odds, the skills-led initiative worked. Global Foundries, a giant based in Singapore, literally half way around the world, started manufacturing in Malta starting in 2009 and had invested a total of $15 billion in its manufacturing complex by 2018. The company created more than 3,000 jobs in Malta. A complete set of suppliers such as

Applied Materials also moved into the region to support Global Foundries, creating many more jobs.

The lesson is that leadership focused on one industry at the regional or local level, supported by state and federal funds but not controlled by those levels of government, is the best formula for growth and competitiveness.

A second model I have studied is the Cuyahoga Community College (Tri-C) in Cleveland, Ohio.[3] The reason it works so well, and the reason that the for-profit private colleges failed so spectacularly, is that the staff of Tri-C meets with business leaders who are looking for certain types of workers. It creates classes on the basis of what the employers need. The companies may send executives or representatives to teach from time to time and may provide equipment that is slightly outdated and no longer of use on the shop floor but is still valuable in training and retraining. Employers are able to hire students as apprentices over a summer, say, and watch a young person's development, contributing to very solid hiring decisions. In sharp contrast, the for-profit private colleges had little contact with employers and did not equip their students with the skills that were in demand.

The models that work are abundantly clear but not enough regions have developed them. One problem has been chaos in the federal government's training and retraining programs. The Government Accountability Office reported in 2011 that the federal government had 47 job training programs reporting to nine different agencies.[4] Most of the programs are overlapping and under-funded. The two primary departments involved are Education and Labor, which are notoriously bureaucratic and ineffective. We need to fix this problem by creating one entity that has clear authority to fund and manage training and re-training.

The new department or office could work with any
industry that wishes its help, but it should have a particularly
tight linkage with the Office of Strategic Technologies. If one
arm of the government is working to establish new
technologies, it makes sense that another arm is trying to
provide it with the human capital it needs. That's not
Communism. It's the way many advanced economies in East
Asia and Europe try to support the emergence of new
industries.

* * *

A renewed dedication to upskilling and reskilling is
part and parcel of any serious effort to encourage more
American companies to "reshore" or "backshore," meaning
bringing home manufacturing from China to American shores.
The shift of millions of jobs offshore started in earnest in the
1980s. CEOs such as Nike's Phil Knight recognized that they
could tap much lower wages in East Asia primarily and offer
products in the American market that would be much cheaper
than otherwise possible. There were other subtexts, of course.
One was that offshoring would help moderate union demands
for higher wages. Another was the belief that offshoring would
create vibrant economies elsewhere, which would serve broader
American strategic interests. "Globalization" was seen as a
positive thing in many quarters.

But since the whole push offshore to China and
elsewhere began, labor costs have increased dramatically in
China, while remaining fairly steady in the United States.
Other costs of transportation and coordination have mounted,
as companies had to send executive and engineers on extended
journeys through Asia to manage their production facilities.

The cost equation has shifted in other ways—electricity is now cheaper in some parts of the United States than it is in China.

All this has led to a broad rethinking of the offshore push of yesteryear. One of the more intriguing results is that some companies are bringing manufacturing back to the United States. I've spoken with CEOs who have done it or attempted to do it and the No. 1 problem they face is that they cannot find a work force with appropriate skills. There are not enough Americans who know how to make things, particularly in a highly automated setting. The rule of thumb has been that if an American manufacturer shifts 10 jobs to China, it may take 15 to 20 Chinese workers to do the same work because they are less trained at performing multiple tasks. But if the manufacturer brings the production home, it is certain to be highly automated. Perhaps only three or four jobs "come home."

The man who has done more than anyone else to spotlight the issue of reshoring is Harry C. Moser, who founded a non-profit organization called the Reshoring Initiative.[5] For Moser, the cause is personal. His grandfather was a foreman at the Singer sewing machine plant in Elizabeth, New Jersey and his father ran the factory, the largest Singer plant in the world, at some point. Harry himself worked there for five or six summers. Now, of course, it is all gone.

He's a believer in the importance of manufacturing, which not every public policy intellectual is. When General Motors and Chrysler went bankrupt in 2009, many voices urged the government to simply let the automakers fail and allow Japanese or Korean competitors to take over. There was no reason American auto manufacturers needed to survive. "The people who say manufacturing doesn't matter are stupid," the plain-spoken Moser offers. "We've had big-time economists say, 'We don't care whether you are doing computer chips or potato chips or we don't care whether you're doing manufacturing or have a hotel or a restaurant. It's all the same.' That's nuts." His point is that manufacturing can be very high value and innovative, with the economic effects ricocheting throughout a region. That's called the multiplier effect. A restaurant or a dry cleaner just cannot compete with that. Business schools, which are educating future business leaders, need to revisit their curricula to examine whether they are encouraging short-term financial results and sacrificing longer-term economic and technological gains that manufacturing often represents.

Moser's Reshoring Initiative tracks all announcements made by U.S. companies about their manufacturing plans and has created the best database of information about reshoring. He also offers tools to companies to help them calculate the complete costs of running a factory abroad or outsourcing manufacturing to a contractor. With costs rising in China and in view of all the hidden "soft costs" of coordinating supply chains and sending executives and engineers on extended trips, Moser has helped convince some companies to reshore.

But it's just beginning. "We are attracting a lot back from China. In 2017, 170,000 manufacturing jobs were announced to come back from offshore to the United States and specifically about a third of that was coming back from China," Moser told me. He is based in Sarasota, FL.

That's a tiny fraction of the millions of jobs that left American shores. Moser believes it is feasible to bring back 25 percent of the manufacturing that left. "From looking at the data, we conclude that something like 25 percent of what's offshore, including in China, would come back if the companies do the math properly." Doing the math properly means adding up all the costs and weighing the risks and benefits of offshore manufacturing.

"To get that 25 percent back, we'd be lucky to get it back within 10 years," Moser said. "There are not enough skilled workers, toolmakers, precision machinists, and chemical technicians. There's just barely enough to support the work we do now. If we increased manufacturing by 10, 20, 30 percent, it would be impossible in the short term. There are just not enough people. It's going to take decades to change society's view of manufacturing and develop apprentice programs and get more smart kids going into those fields."

Being an old-fashioned guy, Moser believes there are security implications for a country that depends on other countries, he estimates, for more than 50 percent of the things it consumes.

If there were greater military tensions with China, "you think they are going to ship us shoes and uniforms for our military?" he asks. "Where are we going to get the computer chips and the microprocessors and the computers to run our economy? It would be one thing for Switzerland to not be self-sufficient because they are tiny. But we are the arsenal of democracy. We need to keep the sea lanes open. We need strong manufacturing and we need some measure of self-sufficiency to be able to survive as we did in World War I and World War II."

Gearing up a manufacturing work force would require some tough decisions. "You need three things—bodies, minds and training," he says. "There are millions of people who have dropped out of the work force because they didn't think they could find a job or they are living on welfare and getting along. For some people, if they can be reasonably comfortable, they'd rather not work. I'd make it less than reasonably comfortable."

A final piece of the puzzle, says Moser, is reaching into high schools and letting teachers and counselors understand that not everyone needs to go to a four-year college and that it is possible to live a good life by working in manufacturing, which has higher wages than many other types of work. "If counselors and teachers know that jobs are coming back, they can say, 'Yes, Susie, why don't you become a welder, not a librarian?'"

Moser sees progress as high schools and community colleges re-introduce shop-oriented classes. They are more expensive to build and maintain than say, teaching English as a second language, because they require thousands of dollars' worth of machines and computers. Students also could be injured, which requires careful management. And he sees more companies starting apprenticeship programs, modeled on the German system. Both the Obama and Trump administrations have supported this effort. These programs allow an employer to get to know individual students and chart their development over a period of time. When they do get hired, it is an informed decision. Everybody wins.

But it starts with kids in high schools being encouraged to think of manufacturing as a solid life choice. "Manufacturing in general too often gets the bottom of the pyramid when it comes to workers. You need the middle and upper middle of the pyramid, and not just the bottom of the pyramid, to go into manufacturing."

A sweeping vision that would take decades to achieve? Absolutely. But it has taken decades to dig ourselves into our current hole.

* * *

Part of the national strategy should be to re-establish at least a modest consumer electronics sector, including computers. For decades, we relied on a model in which we outsourced the making of every computer and every cell phone to someone or some place outside the United States. In the majority of cases, that meant China. And now, belatedly, we realize that has created a vulnerability. This would take years to achieve because the entire consumer electronics infrastructure in the United States was wiped out.

Apple has a great deal at stake because it relies on Terry Gou, chief executive of the Taiwan-based company FoxConn, to make most of Apple's products at factories in China. Gou made a big splashy announcement in 2017[6] that Foxconn would build a $10 billion manufacturing complex in Wisconsin to make liquid crystal display screens for flat screen televisions and hire 13,000 workers. The company broke ground in 2018 but then in early 2019 abruptly announced it was going to turn the facility into a research and development facility. After a telephone conversation between Trump and Gou, FoxConn said it would, in fact, build the factory. Apple should make sure the project is realized because it needs to diversify its manufacturing base. But it's also critically important for the entire United States to re-establish a complete ecosystem of suppliers and customers on U.S. soil.

The Pentagon has an enormous self-interest in re-establishing at least a modest electronics sector. It could be part of the solution by starting to help its entire supplier base establish security and self-sufficiency, starting perhaps with the Mountain Pass rare earth mine.

Many of these proposals may seem radical. They certainly cost money. Where will that come from? We will have to ask ourselves tough questions about spending trillions of dollars in military operations around the world in places that suffer from intractable war, about supporting able-bodied people with welfare, food stamps and disability pay, about having more people in prison than any other country in the

Western world, about building physical border walls in an era of cyber warfare, and about a tax system that allows billionaires to dodge taxes. There is a sensible middle path.

The response to Chinese government activities on our soil, as well as on other fronts, will require long-term thinking on the part of political leaders and it will require business leaders to break out of the mindset that their only obligation is to their shareholders and quarterly profits. The philosophy that must take hold is that CEOs have multiple "stakeholders," including customers, suppliers, employees and their communities and that the interests of all these stakeholders should be respected over time. That list includes national security. If maximizing quarterly profits means knowingly operating with computer systems that have been compromised, that's a terrible idea. The systems must be upgraded and protected at whatever the cost over a period of time.

All these urgent challenges—stronger defenses, new governmental structures, a technology strategy, upskilling the workforce and reshoring manufacturing—are connected and all relate directly to the China challenge. They cannot be addressed by flipping a switch. They require sustained institutional focus for the foreseeable future—for decades. They are precisely the opposite of imposing barriers and borders and tariffs against China and the rest of the world. They would represent a strengthening of the American economic model.

Our economy does not necessarily have to remain larger than China's but we need to maintain and enhance our technological clout for the benefit of as many people as possible so that we maintain at least as much independence and credibility as Japan and Germany have today. If we can improve our economic model in response to the challenge that

China represents, we can maintain our way of life and our values even if their economy becomes larger. It is not the size of the economy that matters as much as its sophistication. But to hold our own on the technological and economic front, we also have to win the soft war.

15 Winning the "Soft War"

Americans, as a whole, have been slow learners when it comes to China. The business community was quick to learn how to operate in China and has been doing so for decades. Academics and government officials also developed real expertise. But even relatively well-educated Americans today, in general, do not understand much more about China than they did when Deng Xiaoping toured the United States and donned a Texan cowboy hat in February 1979, at the moment I was arriving in Hong Kong.

I suspect Americans have not wanted to learn or have not felt the need to learn about China because they assumed that our values and ideals were so powerful that ultimately the Chinese would accept them. The reason the image of Deng in the cowboy hat became so famous was that it made us wonder, will the Chinese take on American ways? It's the classic American attitude toward immigrants. "They'll learn."

But China's government, particularly under President Xi's leadership, is determined to defend its own values. It does not respect our values or our institutions. In fact, Xi has argued that Chinese Communism is a superior system. And he has geared up an impressive government-and party-wide effort to help it prevail in the world.

FBI Director Wray had a particularly interesting insight in testifying before Congress. I suspect not many people would understand the full implications. He said China's challenge to us is not just a "whole-of-government" threat but also a "whole-of-society" challenge.[1] That means Xi has set clear goals and is pushing millions of Chinese down the path he has chosen for them. The only way to respond to that, Wray said, is a "whole-of-society response by us."

I think that simply understanding the Chinese government's strategy, as it plays out in the United States, will create resistance to it. We will no longer be as naïve and completely open, assuming that the latest newcomers will buy into our system and our values. University leaders will no longer express amazement that Chinese students are being targeted by Chinese diplomats or intelligence agencies, either when they are still at the university or when they have graduated. The NIH will no longer simply assume that all Chinese professors and scientists are playing by American rules. Americans will learn the difference between advertorials sponsored by *People's Daily* and actual content prepared by the staff of *The New York Times*.

Broadly speaking, we need better mechanisms to create long-term China policies that are not subjected to electoral uncertainty and that encompass the full range of our points of engagement and conflict with the Chinese party-state. What happens internationally is connected to what happens within our own borders, but our China-facing governmental mechanisms are set up to concentrate on China's international actions, not what the party-state is doing inside the United States. There is a thicket of agencies that already exist, but it seems we need some type of a China Council at the White House level consisting of wise voices who cut across the different domains—foreign policy, intelligence, defense, corporate and technology, and university and academic experts—and who can monitor China's actions inside the United States as well as elsewhere in an integrated, holistic manner. This would be part and parcel of trying to establish and institutionalize an all-of-government and perhaps an all-of-society response.

If there are other bodies that can be consolidated into a China Council, that would be better than creating another bureaucracy. The China Council should be de-politicized and terms for its members should be long-term. The council should be encouraged to speak truth to decision-makers a way of countering the revolving door effect in Washington and elsewhere. Its moral authority would be as important as its bureaucratic power. It's not good enough to have an annual report from a body such as the U.S.-China Economic and Security Review Commission. It needs to be full-time job.

We need more funding for Chinese studies at U.S. high schools and colleges. We need to develop greater intellectual leadership on all the issues at stake. We need more Americans to study Chinese, as difficult as it is, and we need more students to go to China to learn, perhaps at the campuses of American universities there. It's much easier to learn Mandarin while immersed in the culture than it is in the United States. At present, there are only about 13,000 American students studying in China.[2] Why not set a target of 100,000? That would not be a statement of surrender. It would be a statement that we are getting serious. Taiwan is also an excellent place to study Chinese. As a society, we need to turn and face China, as President Obama's "pivot to Asia" once suggested. But the United States made only superficial progress in that direction.

If a university has a professor who is denied a visa to travel to China for legitimate research, the president of that university should elevate the issue to the highest levels and decline to cooperate further with any party-state entities. The president must not continue to accept Chinese funding while allowing his or her professors to be shut out of China.

Universities and high schools should shut down their Confucius Institutes if they cannot sign transparent, public contracts that adhere to American law, not Chinese law, which was one step recommended by the Chinese Influence & American Interests report.

And as the Wilson Center report recommended, universities should do a better job of communicating among themselves and with federal authorities about Chinese diplomatic pressures on them. That is clearly crossing a line in terms of interference in our domestic affairs.

Chinese-Americans should be careful about becoming too involved with unification societies supported by the Chinese party-state in many U.S. cities because they could lead them down a path that puts them at odds with American interests or creates the appearance of such.

In general, we must have a discussion about the Chinese living among us. This is incredibly sensitive—so sensitive that the Congressional Asian Pacific American Caucus declined to even discuss my request for an interview. But the burning question remains: How can we work with the leaders of the Chinese-American community to devise ways of embracing all that is good about having Chinese and Chinese-Americans living in the United States while addressing some of the obvious abuses this book has detailed?

As I have stressed, there is a wide continuum of Chinese and Chinese-Americans living in America. An entire race should not and cannot be criminalized. The key characteristics of the Chinese who have been arrested for espionage or penetrating our institutions were that they were born on the mainland, have family there, were educated at American universities and went to work in American technology companies or government agencies. If they travelled internationally frequently, that has been a possible sign that they were meeting with co-conspirators or officials of the MSS and its provincial affiliates.

The best people to help spot these practices are Chinese-Americans, who understand more about the language and culture than Americans of other ethnicities do. The Chinese-American community, in short, could be one of our best tools in shutting down the practices we find reprehensible on our own soil. Chinese or Chinese-Americans working for American news organizations have been particularly effective in explaining patterns of Chinese governmental activity on U.S. soil that most American reporters would miss.

The possibility of harming Chinese-Americans was perhaps the most contentious one among the academics who wrote the Chinese Influence & American Interests report, leading one of the original leaders of the project to issue a dissent. Speaking for the majority, Orville Schell and Larry Diamond, wrote in an afterword, "Just because the Chinese Communist Party presumes that all ethnic Chinese (wherever they may reside) still owe some measure of loyalty to the Chinese motherland does not mean that they are collectively in possession of compromised loyalty to their adopted home or place of study." The fact that China's party-state has increased its influence peddling in the United States "should not be viewed as an invitation to a McCarthy era-like reaction against Chinese in America."

In a dissenting opinion, Susan Shirk, from the University of California at San Diego, said she feared "an anti-Chinese version of the Red Scare that would put all ethnic Chinese under a cloud of suspicion." For that reason, she concluded, the harm to American society of overreacting to Chinese-Americans "is greater than that caused by Chinese influence seeking." She did not mention the Chinese government's theft of technology or its penetration of American institutions because those actions were largely beyond the scope of the Chinese Influence study.

For readers who consider it racist to even ask the question of how we combat espionage and penetrations by Chinese agents living among us, answer these questions: Is it not more sinister that China's party-state assumes that all ethnic Chinese must be loyal to Beijing and must allow themselves to be "weaponized" and therefore made vulnerable to arrest or humiliation? Where is the respect for their right to live their own lives? Who has the moral responsibility for creating a situation in which Chinese-Americans could be suspected? The answer is clear to me: the Chinese party-state has victimized, and continues to victimize, some Chinese and Chinese-Americans living in the United States.

* * *

We need to better understand the power of words and ideas, which may seem like a rash statement in today's political and cultural environment with social media studded with "deep fakes," meaning falsified audio and video clips. But we need to enhance our ability to recognize propaganda and falsehoods when we see them and to understand the source of information that is presented to us. This is part of the challenge of reviving American journalism as a moderating force in our society, not a divisive force. We have all experienced the instantaneous communication joys of Facebook, Google and Twitter, but as time passes, we are learning more about how they have confused us as a nation.

The Internet and social media, once greeted as liberators, have proven to be a source of political manipulation and an invasion of privacy. Now, analyzing the patterns of Chinese activity, we see that the Internet has opened us to massive, consistent and deep penetration of our institutions and our lives. With 800 million Internet-users and an urban population who have embraced all things digital, there appears to be an imbalance between China's digital capabilities and our own. Encouraging more of our young to pursue STEM educations is part of the answer. But individuals must protect their own systems and those of the companies where they work. Individually, they should strengthen their personal systems by going to two-step authentification log-ins and buying protection against viruses and malware.

We need to allow the pendulum swing back from its current position of denying expertise, a trend that has been widely chronicled. Tom Nichols, from the Naval War College, wrote a very fine book in 2017 called *The Death of Expertise: The Campaign Against Established Knowledge and Why It Matters.*[3] He described how Internet users feel they can learn everything they need to know online, so why read a book written by "elitists?" "All voices, even the most ridiculous, demand to be taken with equal seriousness," he wrote. Of course, that cheapens the national debate on any issue, particularly one as complex as China's strategy in the United States.

Michiko Kakutani, of the *The New York Times*, wrote a similar tome in 2018 called, *The Death of Truth: Notes on Falsehood in The Age of Trump.*[4] She lamented the disappearance of verifiable facts that can be accepted by all participants in America's political and cultural wars. Without such facts, "there can be no rational debate over policies, no substantive means of evaluating candidates for political office, and no way to hold elected officials accountable to the people," she wrote. "Without truth, democracy is hobbled." We need to be able to talk about the facts of China's involvement in the United States without turning the discussion into a witch hunt.

Solutions to all these issues, of course, are difficult. Individuals must become more sophisticated about what news and entertainment they consume and become more skeptical about the sources of extreme views presented to them. It must be a society-wide response. Every institution in American business and society that touches China should ask whether it has sufficient information about China and the nature of the relationship that a particular American company or institution is building with China. Does the relationship build dependency? Is it leading you into activities that are not in keeping with the national interest? The Chinese Influence & American Interests report contains valuable information about the different Chinese institutions and entities active in America at the state and local level.

Responding forcefully is partly a question of time and money allocation. Americans spend so much time and money playing fantasy football, betting on Lotto, playing Solitaire on their smart phones, watching videos of Baby Sharks, and looking at pictures of pet chihuahuas on Instagram. An incredible 100 million people were said to have watched the most recent Superbowl. Imagine if just a fraction of that time and money was instead spent on reading and talking about China-related issues as they affect us in our daily lives. That doesn't mean debating the fine points of Ching Dynasty history. It means talking about the origins of the goods we buy, education and training, staying ahead in key technologies, and other issues I've spotlighted.

Ultimately, and this also seems improbable at the moment, we have to recognize that we are not governing ourselves well, creating opportunities for the Chinese to play in the shadows. Shutting down the federal government is just stupid whichever political party is held responsible. If we Americans are focused on destroying each other in the political combat zone, we create an environment that makes outside interference infinitely easier. Imagine what China's party-state strategists (as well as those of Russia, North Korea and Iran) must be thinking about the vaunted American democracy proving unable to keep its own government running.

My hope is that the shock of what the Chinese are achieving on our own shores will be great enough that it results in Americans coming together to face a common challenge without resulting in a burst of racist and xenophobic persecution. If we can't clean up the swamp in Washington and in many state capitals, a centrally focused, wealthy competitor will be able to win the contest without firing a shot, which Sun Tsu called the "highest art of war." If no one thinks of the national interest, beyond their own parochial and institutional interests, how can the nation long endure?

Paul Ryan's comments were revealing as he stepped down as Speaker of the House. He called the political process "broken."[5] And then he added: "Outrage has become a brand and, as with anything that gets marketed, it gets scaled up. It is just emotional pabulum fed from a trough of outrage. It's exhausting. It saps meaning from politics, and it discourages good people from pursuing public service."

Overcoming that will require an effort by Americans of different ideological and political stripes to come together to agree on a new political center. What logical, sensible actions should the United States take in the technology field, in retraining and training, and in reshoring? There are always going to be the hot-button issues of immigration, race relations, gender, guns, abortion, school prayer and others. Those issues have been with us for decades and probably will remain with us forever. The key is to not allow them to deny us the ability to create a pragmatic center. News outlets, websites and cable channels that sell pure rage should be shunned; those that offer reasonable middle grounds, if any are left, should be embraced. "Click bait," the use of provocative headlines to attract viewers to stories that don't live up to the headlines, are one sure sign of a site that should not be trusted.

I am not proposing a return to the warm and fuzzy era of *Ozzie and Harriet* or *Father Knows Best*. I recognize the deep economic and technological forces that have transformed American life and that will continue to do so. The technological revolution of recent years is just gathering steam for further sustained radical change.

What I do believe, however, is that Americans have traditionally enjoyed certain assets—a balanced media, trusted far-sighted leaders, strong universities, institutional flexibility, love of country, and a thirst for innovation—that should be allowed to sustain us in contending with Chinese government intrusiveness. That's why efforts by the Chinese party-state to undermine our faith in our own institutions are so dangerous. Why should we cooperate in assaulting our own institutions? That seems to be what has happened in Britain as it wrestled with the question of leaving the European Union. Trust among British leaders and institutions has vanished. There are no facts, only insults.

There is absolutely no reason for a U.S. military confrontation against China. The two countries have, in effect, merged their economies. Military conflict would be incredibly destructive and perhaps not successful from our perspective. We have experienced the power of China's population in a land war in Korea, losing tens of thousands of soldiers. China also lent support to North Vietnam, which resulted in many more American losses. Any conflict today would be more likely to be in the skies, on the seas and in cyberspace, but it could be just as deadly as a land war. We do not need abrupt breaks in our relations with China, just long-term, gradual steps on multiple fronts— for as far as the eye can see. That's part and parcel of taking a longer-term strategic view and breaking out of our short-term obsession with tweets and polls and the latest rally on Wall Street.

Friends and associates who have spoken to me about the subject of China's role in America, or read drafts of this book, sometimes tell me that it's a lost cause. The Chinese have won. Americans don't have the will to resist. We just have to accept the inevitable.

If that is your conviction, then it's time for you to accept the dragon's claws in America. Accept the form of colonization that the Chinese party-state is attempting to impose. You have to accept that the best ideas in America will get stolen and jobs created elsewhere. Accept that our governmental institutions may be compromised and our universities neutralized. Our computer systems have been thoroughly compromised. Our think tanks will serve foreign masters. Accept that Chinese state-backed media and a China-infatuated Hollywood shape your children's and grandchildren's perceptions.

I, for one, am not ready to accept any of that. I believe we have the time and I believe that the distinct American combination of democracy and capitalism can once again rise to the challenge. As an economic patriot, I have a fierce sense of conviction that there is no other choice but to make a determined effort to blunt the dragon's claws.

16 Summary of Recommendations

From chapter 12, Harden the Targets:

—The Department of Justice and the FBI must make sure there is no lingering harm from the 10-year betrayal by Joey Chun.

—All government agencies involved in major Information Technology upgrades must assume that China's party-state will attempt to penetrate their new systems.

—The Pentagon, particularly the Navy, must move swiftly to eliminate IT vulnerabilities.

—Keep Huawei and ZTE out of the push to 5G telecommunications networks in the United States and impose stringent inspections of all imported equipment.

—Key government agencies have to accelerate and improve their understanding of new, emerging technologies so they know what to protect and what not to protect.

—Companies of all sizes must embrace intrusion detection systems and employ skilled operators who can detect attacks. One compromised company in a supply chain can lead to compromises in all partner companies.

—CEOs must not continue to operate IT systems they believe may have been compromised by Chinese government hackers. It is worth the time and money to fix the underlying problem. National security is at stake.

—Companies that suspect they have insider threats should cooperate with federal authorities rather than trying to hide or conceal the problem.
—Companies should develop insider threat programs that scrutinize all areas of risk and do not single out Chinese or Chinese-Americans on the basis of their ethnicity.
—The scientific community, including the National Institutes of Health, needs to rethink its completely open approach to research. Steps must be taken to prevent China's government from fraudulently obtaining cutting-edge technology.
—The number of Chinese students in the inner sanctums of research and development labs must be gradually reduced.

From chapter 13, Toward a Winning Technology Strategy:

—Use the existing White House Office of Science and Technology Policy as the basis to create a new Office of Strategic Technologies that would have responsibilities for protecting existing technologies against Chinese government attack but also would help nurture newer technologies targeted by Beijing.
—Declare that technology clusters are "global centers of excellence," which would galvanize all members of these "ecosystems" to improve collaboration among themselves but also with federal agencies. The Office of Strategic Technologies could coordinate federal spending in a way that enhances the ability of these clusters to excel.
—Private investors in these global centers of excellence would enjoy tax benefits.

—Boost federal R&D spending for universities, research institutes, national weapons labs and others and encourage them to speed up the commercialization of their new ideas.

—The Office of Strategic Technologies could broker deals to help struggling but strategic industries such as rare earths, where a single American company is competing, and it could help identify crucial gaps in supply chains for crucial technologies.

From chapter 14, Upskilling and Reshoring:

—Create a clear educational infrastructure for training and retraining workers, relying heavily on community colleges, and consolidate the 47 different federal programs spread among nine agencies.

—This new training and retraining agency should coordinate with the Office of Strategic Technologies to anticipate the skills that are going to be in demand.

—Business schools should re-examine their curricula to determine whether they are training future corporate leaders to think only in terms of short-term financial gains while sacrificing the value of manufacturing on U.S. soil.

—Encourage high schools and vocational schools to help educate students. Not everyone should go to a four-year college or university. It's possible to create a living and find professional satisfaction as a welder or quality technician.

—Expand use of German-style apprentice programs that encourage high school students to work during summer vacations at a particular company.

—Seek to re-establish at least a modest consumer electronics industry in the United States, to ease dependence on computers and smart phones made in China.

From chapter 15, Winning the "Soft War"

—Recognize that the United States needs a "whole-of-society" response to the Chinese government's activities on American soil. Anyone who has a point of contact must educate themselves to understand how the party-state uses carrots and sticks to undermine the independence of crucial institutions.

—Recognize propaganda emanating from Chinese state-owned information sources and become more sophisticated about understanding the origin and validity of news derived from smart phones and the Internet.

—Create a standing China Council consisting of well-respected China experts in industry, government, academia, science and finance who can develop an overview of all aspects of the U.S.-Chinese relationship and offer clear, consistent advice to American leaders of all stripes and persuasians.

—Increase funding for Chinese studies at American high schools and universities. Set a goal of sending 100,000 students to China to study.

—University presidents should not maintain economic ties with Chinese entities if their professors are denied visas to travel to China to study.

—Universities and high schools should shut down Confucius Institutes funded by China's Ministry of

Education if they cannot publicly disclose their contracts and base them on U.S. law, not Chinese law.

—Chinese-Americans should be careful about becoming too involved in unification societies the Chinese government has established across the United States.

—We should seek to embrace Chinese-Americans who can help news organizations, law enforcement agencies and other organizations to understand and stop practices by the Chinese government that are not in keeping with American interests.

—Work strenuously to prevent an effort to stop Chinese government abuses from becoming a hysterical campaign against all Chinese-Americans.

—Establish a new political center to concentrate on the issues that China's interference poses and prevent identity issues of race and gender from permanently dividing us.

—Work hard to establish the notion that "economic patriotism" unites us as we attempt to improve the American economic model so that it can out-compete China.

ACKNOWLEDGMENTS

Long-time friends Tom and Leah Nathans Spiro traveled to Australia where they experienced that nation's debate about Chinese nationals attempting to procure political influence there. Upon returning, Leah told me about Clive Hamilton's book, "The Silent Invasion," and encouraged me to examine Chinese government activities in the United States. At first, I was skeptical. But soon after starting reporting and researching, it became clear that an even more sophisticated pattern of Chinese activity was unfolding on American soil (and I presume, by the way, that the Chinese party-state is engaged in some version of these practices in every country around the world where it has interests.)

Another long-time friend, Pat Oster, the former legal affairs editor at Bloomberg, suggested I use court documents in my research. That proved to be a most valuable line of inquiry.

My agent, Alan Morrell, provided wise counsel and sage advice at crucial moments.

And my most heartfelt thanks go to my wife, Rita Sevell, who has survived five books in 10 years of marriage. Having a psychotherapist on call is a privilege every author should enjoy. I am eternally grateful to her and deeply in love.

Reference Notes

Chapter 1

1   Holstein, William J. "How I Survived a Cyber Attack
     by the Chinese Military." *Chief Executive* magazine.
     January/February 2016.

2   The White House, Office of the Press Secretary.
     Remarks by President Obama and President Xi of the
     People's Republic of China in Joint Press Conference.
     Sept. 25, 2015.
     https://obamawhitehouse.archives.gov/the-press-
     office/2015/09/25/remarks-president-obama-and-presid
     ent-xi-peoples-republic-china-joint. Sept. 25, 2015

3   Office of the United States Trade Representative,
     Executive Office of the President. "Findings of the
     investigation into China's acts, policies, and practices
     related to technology transfer, intellectual property, and
     innovation under Section 301 of the Trade Act of 1974.
     March 22, 2018

4   Yuan, Li. *The New York Times*. "A Billion Reasons to
     Use WeChat in China." Jan. 10, 2019.

5   U.S. Department of Justice, Office of Public Affairs.
     "Two Chinese Hackers Associated With the Ministry of
     State Security Charged with Global Computer
     Intrusion Campaigns Targeting Intellectual Property
     and Confidential Business Information." Dec. 20,
     2018. https://www.justice.gov/opa/pr/two-chinese-
     hackers-associated-ministry-state-security-charged-glob
     al-computer-intrusion

6   United States District Court, Southern District of New York. United States of America vs. Zhu Hua and Zhang Shilong. Dec. 17, 2018.
https://www.justice.gov/opa/press-release/file/1121706/download

7   The *Wall Street Journal,* "U.S. Steps Up Hacking Fight." Dec. 21, 2018

8   Justice Department, *op cit.*

9   Robertson, Jordan and Riley, Michael. Bloomberg *Bloomberg Businessweek.* "The Big Hack: How China Used a Tiny Chip to Infiltrate U.S. Companies." Oct. 8, 2018

10 Baron, Ethan. The San Jose Mercury News. "H-1B: Foreign citizens make up three three-quarters of Silicon Valley tech workforce, report says." Jan. 17, 2018.

11 McCartney, Robert and Siddiqui, Faiz. *The Washington Post.* "Could a Chinese-made Metro car spy on us? Many experts say yes." January 8, 2019

Chapter 2

1   Lyons, Brendan J. *Times Union.* "GE engineer charged with stealing turbine technology." Aug. 1, 2018

2   Viswanatha, Aruna and O'Keefe, Kate, *The Wall Street Journal,* "Prior to Hack, Equifax Feared Chinese Spying." Sept. 3, 2018

3   United States District Court for the Northern District of California, United States of America v. United Microelectronics Corporation, et al. Filed Sept. 27, 2018

4   Assistant Attorney General Brian A. Benczkowski of the Criminal Division Delivers Remarks Regarding Chinese Economic Espionage, Nov. 1, 2018

5   Benner, Katie. *The New York Times.* "Chinese Officer Brought to U.S. on Spy Charge." Oct. 10, 2018

6   United States District Court Southern District of Ohio, Western Division. https://www.justice.gov/opa/press-release/file/1099876/download

7   Ministry of State Security (China), Wikipedia

8   Vice President Mike Pence's Remarks on the Administration's policy Towards China, the Hudson Institute, Oct. 4, 2018

9   Yam, Kimberly. HuffPost. "Chinese-American Scientist Wrongly Accused of Spying Gets Job Back." April 27, 2018

10   Rappeport, Alan. *The New York Times.* "U.S. Blocks Chinese Firm Over Tech Security Issues. Oct. 30, 2018

11   United States District Court for the Western District of Washington at Seattle. "United States of America v. Huawei Device Co. and Huawei Device USA."

Chapter 3

1   Crawford, Terry. *The Chronicle of Higher Education.* "Why Chinese Students Aren't a Threat." April 30, 2018

2   Hackman, Michelle and Belkin, Douglas. *The Wall Street Journal.* "Schools Get Fewer Overseas Students." Nov. 14, 2018

3   Hanlon, Philip J. and Slaughter, Matthew J. *The Wall Street Journal* editorial page. & "Chinese Students Help America Innovate." Nov. 13, 2018

4   Karni, Anne. Politico. "Trump rants behind closed doors with CEOs." Aug. 8, 2018

5   Wessel, Michael. Testimony before the joint Oversight and Research and Technology Subcommittees, House

Science, Space and Technology Committee, April 11, 2018

6   Cheng, Yangyang. The ChinaFile. "How to Be a Chinese Scientist without Being China's Scientist." Nov. 27, 2018

7   Priestap, E.W. Testimony before the Committee on The Judiciary, U.S. Senate. Dec. 5, 2018

8   Yuan, Li. *The Wall Street Journal.* "Beijing Recruits in U.S. To Narrow Tech Gap." June 27, 2018

9   Wray, Chris. Testimony before the U.S. Senate Select Committee on Intelligence, Feb. 13, 2018

10 Facher, Lev. STATNews. "NIH is investigating researchers who might have failed to disclose contributions from foreign governments." Aug. 23, 2018

11 Facher, Lev. STATNews, "NIH report scrutinizes role of China in theft of U.S. scientific research." Dec. 13, 2018

12 Pear, Robert, *The New York Times*, "U.S. Officials Warn Health Researchers: China May Be Trying To Steal Your Data." Jan. 7, 2019

Chapter 4

1   Holstein, William J. "The Next American Economy: Blueprint For a Real Recovery." Chapter One. Walker, 2011

2   Bathon, Michael. Bloomberg. Wanxiang Wins U.S. Approval to Buy Battery Maker A123. Jan. 30, 2013

3   Office of the United States Trade Representative, Executive Office of the President. "Findings of the investigation into China's acts, policies, and practices related to technology transfer, Intellectual Property,

and innovation under Section 301 of the Trade Act of 1974. March 22, 2018

Chapter 5

1 U.S.-China Economic and Security Review Commission, 2018 Report to Congress. November 2018.
2 Jiang, Ethel. Business Insider. "Goldman Sachs: Chinese tech giants are dominating North America in VC funding for the first time, and it could be the start of an unprecedented boom." Sept. 9, 2018.
3 Fuller, Thomas. *The New York Times.* "The Pleasure and Pain of Being California, the World's 5th-Largest Economy." May 7, 2018
4 Brown, Michael. Defense Innovation Unit Experimental. "China's Technology Transfer Strategy: How Chinese Investments in Emerging Technology Enable A Strategic Competitor to Access the Crown Jewels of U.S. Innovation." January 2018
5 Brown, Michael A. Statement before the House Permanent Select Committee on Intelligence, July 19, 2008
6 Orr, Gordon. McKinsey & Co. "What Can We Expect In China in 2019?" December 2018
7 Spegele, Brian and O'Keeffe, Kate. *The Wall Street Journal.* "Boeing Backs Out of Global IP Satellite Order Financed by China." Dec. 7, 2018
8 Strumpf, Dan and O'Keeffe, Kate, *The Wall Street Journal.* "U.S. Blocks Huawei Unit From Exporting." Jan. 11, 2019

Chapter 6

1	The United States Attorney's Office, Southern District of New York. Press release. "Former FBI Employee Sentenced in Manhattan Federal Court to 24 Months in Prison For Acting As an Agent of China." Jan. 20, 2017

2	The United States Attorney's Office, press release, *op. cit.*

3	United States District Court, Northern District of Illinois, Eastern Division. United States of America v. Ji Chaoqun. Sept. 21, 2018

4	Lubold, Gordon and Volz, Dustin. *The Wall Street Journal.* "Chinese Hackers Breach Navy Data." Dec. 15, 2018

5	Corrigan, Jack. Nextgov. "Hundreds of IT Flaws Leave the Pentagon's Finances at Risk." Jan. 10, 2019

6	The United States Attorney's Office, Eastern District of Virginia. Press release. "Former CIA Officer Charged with Conspiracy to Commit Espionage." May 8, 2018

7	Carvalho, Raquel. *South China Morning Post.* "Jerry Chun Shing Lee spy trial: ex-CIA officer pleads not guilty, will wait a year before trial in US." May 19, 2008

8	Sanger, David E., Perlroth, Nicole, Thrush, Glenn and Rappeport, Alan. *The New York Times.* "Marriott Data Breach Traced to Chinese Hackers." Dec. 12, 2008. See also: Sanger, David E. "Marriott Says Millions of Hacked Passport Numbers Weren't Encrypted." Jan. 5, 2019

9	Porter, Christopher. Lawfare. "In Cyber Warfare, the Front Line Is Everywhere the U.S. Government Isn't." Aug. 24, 2018. See https://www.lawfareblog.com/cyber-warfare-front-line-everywhere-us-government-isnt.

Chapter 7

1 Asia Society, Press Release. "Asia Society Names New Board Leaders." Nov. 1, 2017. See https://asiasociety.org/asia-society-names-new-board-leaders-launches-135m-capital-campaign
2 See www.chinainstitute.org
3 Diamond, Larry and Schell, Orville. Hoover Institution Press. "Chinese Influence & American Interests: Promoting Constructive Vigilance." 2018.
4 See www.ckgsb.edu.cn

Chapter 8

1 Eller, Donnelle. *Des Moines Register.* "Citing Ad in Des Moines Register, Trump Accuses China of Meddling in U.S. Elections." Sept. 26, 2018
2 Kounalakis, Markos. Hoover Institution Press. "Spin Wars and Spy Games: Global Media and Intelligence Gathering." 2018
3 Foarde, Conner. *The Washington Times.* "Author warns state-controlled Chinese, Russian media are supplanting West in media coverage." Aug. 7, 2018
4 O'Keefe, Kate and Viswanatha, Aruna. *The Wall Street Journal.* "U.S. Orders Chinese Outlets To Join Foreign-Agents List." Sept. 19, 2008
5 Mozur, Paul. *The New York Times.* "China Airs Propaganda in the U.S. on Live TV." March 9, 2019
6 Qin, Amy and Carlsen, Audrey. *The New York Times* and *Boston Globe.* "Don't expect a Chinese villain from Hollywood: Beijing attempts to shape nation's global narrative." November 18, 2018

7   Bond, Paul. *The Hollywood Reporter.* "Dalian Wanda
      Scales Back AMC Investment." Sept. 14, 2008

8   Cheng, Dean. Testimony before Committee on the
      Judiciary, U.S. Senate. "The PRC and Intelligence
      Gathering: Unconventional Targets and
      Unconventional Methods." Dec. 12, 2018

Chapter 9

1   Diamond, Schell, op cit.

2   Wang, Jackie. *Dallas News*. "Texas A&M System
      cuts ties with China's Confucius Institutes after
      congressmen's concern over spying." April 5, 2018

3   Lloyd-Damnjanovic, Anastasya. The Wilson Center.
      "A Preliminary Study of PRC Political Influence and
      Interference Activities in American Higher
      Education." 2018

4   Xinhua via *Global Times*, "President Xi urges new
      media outlet to 'tell China stories well.'" Dec. 31,
      2016

5   Zhu, Lia. *China Daily USA*. "US schools setting up
      campuses in China." Jan. 25, 2018

6   Cohen, Jerome. Xinjiang Initiative, Sept. 20, 2018,
      see http://www.jeromecohen.net/jerrys-
      blog/xinjiang-initiative

Chapter 10

1   Parello-Plesner J. Hudson Institute. "The Chinese
      Communist Party's Foreign Interference Operations:
      How the U.S. and Other Democracies Should
      Respond." June 20, 2018

2   Ives, Mike. *The New York Times*. "Chinese Student in

Maryland Is Criticized at Home for Praising U.S."
May 23, 2017

3   Radio Free Asia. "Chinese Secret Police 'Recruit
Students as Agents' to Spy on Activists Overseas."
Jan. 30, 2018. See
https://www.rfa.org/english/news/china/recruit-
01302018110158.html.

4   Zhongsun, Qi, a pseudonym. *Foreign Policy.*
"Chinese Students Protest in America, Face
Danger at Home." May 28, 2018

5   Allen-Ebrahimian, Bethany. The Daily Beast. "China
Built an Army of Influence Agents in the U.S." July
18, 2018

6   Blackwell, Tom. National Post. "'Don't Step Out of
Line:' Confidential Report Reveals How Chinese
Officials Harass Activists in Canada." Jan. 5, 2018

Chapter 11

1   Swanson, Ana and Vogel, Kenneth P. *The New York
Times.* "Faced With Crippling Sanctions, ZTE
Loaded Up on Lobbyists." Aug. 1, 2018

2   Swanson, Vogel, *op cit.*

3   Woo, Stu. *The Wall Street Journal.* "Embatted
Huawei Bulks Up Legal Team." Dec. 18, 2018

4   Mozur, Paul and Zhong, Raymond. *The New York
Times.* "Beijing Has Few Options Against U.S. on
Huawei."Jan 30, 2018

5   Hudson Institute. Remarks by Vice President
Pence on The Administration's Policy Toward
China. Oct. 4, 2018

6   Fish, Isaac Stone. The *Washington Post* opinion page. "A Chinese company's surprising ties to the Brookings Institution." Dec. 7, 2018

Chapter 12

1   H.R. 3359. Cybersecurity and Infrastructure Security Agency Act of 2018. See https://www.congress.gov/bill/115th-congress/house-bill/3359

2   U.S. Strategic Command. USSTRATCOM's New Command and Control Facility Transitions to Phase II. June 12, 2018

3   Miller, Ron. TechCrunch. "What each cloud company could bring to the Pentagon's $10 billion JEDI cloud contract." Sept. 29, 2018

4   Governmental Accountability Office. "DoD Just Beginning to Grapple with Scale of Vulnerabilities." Oct. 9. 2018

5   U.S.-China Economic and Security Review Commission, op cit.

6   Yuan, Li. *The New York Times.* "A New Year in China and Storm Clouds Ahead." Feb. 4, 2019

7   Pancevski, Bojan. *The Wall Street Journal.* "Germany Weighs Ban on Huawei." Jan. 18, 2019

8   Corrigan, Jack. Nextgov. "Lawmakers Introduce Bill to Fight Chinese Tech Theft and Supply Chain Threats." Jan. 4, 2019.

9   Porter, Christopher, Lawfare. *Op cit.*

10 The National Counterintelligence and Security Center. Press release. "National Counterintelligence and Security Center launches campaign to help private industry guard against threats from nation-state actors."

xciv   Mervis, Jeffrey. Sciencemag. "More restrictive U.S. policy on Chinese graduate student visas raises alarm." Jun 11, 2018

Chapter 13

1   Breeden, John. Nextgov. "How a New Law Supports Quantum Computing's Great Leap Forward." Jan. 9, 2019

2   Mervis, Jeffrey. Sciencemag. "U.S. Senate confirms Kevin Droegemeier to lead White House science office." Jan. 3, 2019

3   Kelly, Kevin et al. *BusinessWeek*. "Hot Spots: America's New Growth Regions." Oct. 19, 1992

4   Porter, Michael E. *Harvard Business Review*. "Clusters and the New Economics of Competition." November-December 1998.

5   *Science* magazine. "Trump, Congress approve largest U.S. research spending increase in decade." Mar. 23, 2018

6   Puko, Timothy. *The Wall Street Journal*. "Tariffs Scorch 'Rare Earth' Mine." Nov. 30, 2018

7   Higgins, Tim. *The Wall Street Journal*. "Tesla to Cut Jobs To Lower Prices." Jan. 19, 2019

Chapter 14

1   Long, Heather. *The Washington Post*. "America has a record 7.1 million job openings, making it an advantageous time to ask for a raise." October 16, 2018

2   Saratoga Economic Development Corporation,

"Semiconductor/Advanced Materials & Supply Chain." https://saratogaedc.com/semiconductor-advanced-materials-supply-chain.

3   Holstein, William J. "The Next American Economy." 2011. Chapter 9.

4   General Accountability Office. Report to Congressional Requesters. "Multiple Employment and Training Programs: Providing Information on Colocating Services and Consolidating Administrative Structures Could Promote Efficiencies." January 2011.

5   Moser, Harry. Reshoring Initiative. See www.reshorenow.org.

6   Kitroeff, Natalie. *The New York Times*. "FoxConn Says Wisconsin Factory Plan Is Still a Go." Feb. 2, 2019.

Chapter 15

1   Wray. *Op cit.*

2   Crace, Anton. The PIE News. "Record numbers studying in China, according to new MoE figures." April 30, 2018.

3   Nichols, Thomas M. "The Death of Expertise: The Campaign Against Established Knowledge and Why It Matters." Oxford University Press. 2017

4   Kakutani, Michiko. "The Death of Truth: Notes on Falsehood in The Age of Trump." Tim Duggan Books. 2018

5   Hirschfield Davis, Julie. *The New York Times*. "Ryan Laments 'Broken' Politics that helped cut his speakership short." Dec. 18, 2018

Index

A

Advanced Micro Devices, 66
Affordable Care Act, 71
Al-Jazeera, 109
Alibaba, 47, 65-66, 84
Align Aerospace, 74
Allen-Ebrahimian, Bethany,
    131-132
Amazon, 33, 38, 111
AMC, 114, 214
American Association for the
    Advancement of Science,
    168
American Enterprise
    Institute, 72, 140, 150
Ant Financial, 47
Apple, Inc., 38, 40, 43, 91,
    141-142, 173, 186
APT10 hacking group, 32-
    36, 95, 157
Artificial Intelligence (AI), 1,
    16, 19, 51, 63, 66, 156
Asia Society, 103
AT&T, 153, 154
Aviation Industry
    Corporation of China
    (AVIC), 73, 74

B

Baidu 65, 84
Barnett, Robbie, 120, 122
British Broadcasting Corp.
    (BBC), 109-110

Beijing: as a city 8, 12-15,
    29, 32, 43, 60, 104, 110,
127, 143, as China's
    government 11, 29, 48,
    50, 66, 101, 103, 110,
    112, 126, 133, 145, 194
Berkeley Artificial
    Intelligence Research
    (BAIR), 63
Bing Nano Research Group,
    63, 104
Biotechnology 34, 75, 163,
    167
Black & Decker, 69
Bloomberg BusinessWeek, 8, 17,
    37-40, 95, 152, 168
Bloomberg TV, 110
BMW, 71
Boeing Company, 25, 47, 73-
    75, 85-86, 141
Bossert, Tom, 95
Boston Globe, 112
Brookings Institution, 140-
    141
Brown, Michael, 79-85
Bush, President George
    H.W., 149, 163

C

Campbell, Joseph S., 36-37,
    51-52, 93-94, 97, 99, 160
Cao, Guoqing, 54
Carlsen, Audrey, 112
Carnegie Mellon University,
    46, 167
Carrico, Kevin, 125
Carter, Ashton, 78
Censorship in China, 18,
    131, 164

Center for Strategic and International Studies (CSIS), 68, 105

Central Intelligence Agency (CIA): compromising of China network, 13, 97-100; venture capital arm, 39, 170-172; In comparison with Ministry of State Security, 46; efforts to exert soft power, 132; possible role in rare earths, 178

Chan, Ronnie C., 103

Chen, Sherry, 53-56

Cheng, Dean, 108-109

Cheng, Yangyang, 64

Cheung Kong Graduate School of Business, 103-104

China Aviation Industry General Aircraft (CAIGA), 73

China Daily, 108, 123

China Global Television Network (CGTN), 109-110, 121

China Institute, 103-105

China National Space Administration, 112

China Orient Asset Management, 85

China Railway Rolling Stock Corp. (CRRSC), 43

ChinaFile, 64

Chinese Influence &

American Interests report, 124, 133-134, 192-196

Chinese People's Political Consultative Conference, 103

Chinese Student and Scholar Associations (CSSAs), 129-130

Chronicle of Higher Education, 60

Chrysler, 182

Chu, Rep. Judy, 54

Chun, Kun Shan "Joey," 13-17, 89-93, 151, 201

Cirrus Aircraft, 73

Cisco Systems, 47

Clinton, former President Bill, 163

CNN, 109, 127

Cohen, Jerome, 125

Collins, Frances, 67

Columbia University, 43-44, 60, 116-126

Committee on Foreign Investment in the U.S. (CFIUS), 77, 83-85, 143, 155, 165

Communist Party, China: in Australia, 11; winning the Chinese civil war, 13; role expanding in China under President Xi, 16, 21, 84, 112, 153-154; Chinese students understanding its power, 52; 2017 party congress, 103; role on U.S.

campuses, 121-124; role in liberal democracies, 131-134; support for U.S. hacking, 155; attitude toward all ethnic Chinese, 193

Congress, U.S: possible use of compromised semiconductors, 17, 39; controversy over District of Columbia's Metro system, 44; NIH peer review system being compromised, 67; chartering the Wilson Center, 121; ZTE lobbying effort, 137-143; testimony by Mark Zuckerberg, 157; approval of quantum computing bill, 164; testimony by the FBI's Christopher Wray, 189; Congressional Asian Pacific American Caucus, 54, 192; House Permanent Select Committee on Intelligence, 83; House Science, Space and Technology Committee, 63; Senate Intelligence Committee, 68; Senate Judiciary Committee, 67, 114

Continental Motors, 73-74

Corning Inc., 46

Crawford, Terry, 60-61

Cultural Revolution, 14, 50, 119

Cuyahoga Community College, 180

Cybersecurity and Infrastructure Security Agency Act, 151

D

Daily Beast, 131

Dalai Lama, 113, 124, 127

Dalian Wanda, 75, 114

Danbury Aerospace, 74

Dartmouth College Tuck School of Business, 62

Demers, John, 48

Deng, Xiaoping, 8, 117, 189

Department of Commerce (U.S.), 53-56, 86, 137, 156-160; National Institute of Standards and Technology, 164.

Department of Defense (Pentagon): U.S. Army, 17, 91-93; U.S. Navy, 17, 25, 32-40, 94-95, 152; vulnerable suppliers, 26; use of compromised servers, 39, 152; U.S. Air Force Office of Scientific Research, 63; Joint Chiefs of Staff, 78; securing own systems, 95-96, 173; Joint Enterprise Defense Infrastructure (JEDI), 151; Defense Criminal

Investigative Service, 35; concerns about D.C. Metro buying Chinese subway cars, 43-44; theft of F-22, F-35 designs, 47; Defense Advanced Research Projects Agency (DARPA), 63, 170, 175; concerns about Silicon Valley, 78-82; Defense Innovation Unit, 78-84, 170; Pentagon's systems criticized; 96; revolving door, 145; new Strategic Command center, 151; Joint Enterprise Defense Infrastructure (JEDI), 151; -GAO report on weapon systems vulnerabilities; role in promoting American technologies, 165; rare earths, 171-173; re-establishing American consumer electronics, 186.

Department of Energy, 63, 70-71, 165-176

Department of Homeland Security, 17, 39, 41, 151, 158, 160

Department of Justice, 35, 48-59, 110, 151, 161, 201

Des Moines Register, 108, 115

Diamond, Larry, 119, 194

DRAMs, 47, 55-56

Droegemeier, Kelvin, 166

Drones, 26, 38, 78, 82, 173

Dropbox, 131

Dual use technologies, 27-29, 78, 82

Duke University, 123

E
Economy, Elizabeth, 135

Eikenberry, Gen. Karl, 135

Elemental Technologies, 38

Eli Lilly, Inc., 54

Epic Aircraft, 73

Equifax, 46-47, 53, 99

F
Facebook 131, 157, 194

Federal Acquisition Regulation (FAR), 41

Federal Bureau of Investigation (FBI): Joey Chun case, 13, 17, 89-91, 151; APT10 case, 32-36, 151; GE Turbine case, 45-46; Equifax case, 47; case of Yanjun Xu, 48-49; Sherry Chen case, 53; Thousand Talents Program, 66-67; warning about open academic research, NIH case, 68; Silicon Valley, 81; Ji Chaoqun case, 91-97; Jerry Chun Shing Lee case, 97-98; Confucius Institutes, 119; outreach to research community, 159, 161; internal security checks,

159-160; "whole-of-society" challenge, 189.
Federal Communications Commission, 139
Fifth generation wireless telecommunications networks (5G), 26, 154, 201
FireEye 25-30, 35, 100, 157
Fish, Isaac Stone, 140
Fisker Automotive, 70-72
Foreign Investment Risk Review Modernization Act (FIRRMA), 83
Foreign Policy magazine, 130
Fox News, 109
FoxConn, 186
Fujian Jinhua Integrated Circuit, 47, 55-56
FutureWei Technologies, 86, 141

G
General Dynamics, 26
General Electric (GE), 16, 45-52, 70, 92, 159
General Motors, 141, 182
Glaser, Bonnie, 135
Global IP, 85
Google, 56, 66, 128, 164, 194
Government Accountability Office (GAO), 152, 180
Graham, Sen. Lindsey, 138
Great Firewall, 16
Grotto, Andrew, 39-44, 95-100, 152-154, 159

Gu, Junli, 66
Gu, Saulaiman, 130

H
Hackers 17, 25-46, 81, 94-96, 151- 152, 201
Hamilton, Clive, 11
Hanban, 118-120
Hanlon, Philip J., 62
Hanssen, Richard, 93
Hawaii Tokay International College, 112
He, (Helen) Xiaohui, 132
Heimowitz, James, 105-106
Heritage Foundation, 114
HNA, 75
Hogan Lovells, 137-138
Hollywood 18, 20, 30, 43, 111-114, 144, 199
Home Depot, 141
Hong Kong, 13
Huawei Technologies, 47, 57-59, 86, 139-141, 153-154, 201
Huaying Haitai, 32
Hudson Institute, 129, 140
Hudson Valley Community College 179
HuffPost 53-54
Human Rights Watch 52, 118, 125, 134, 144

I
IBM Corp., 33-35, 46, 72
Illinois Institute of Technology, 92

Information Technology, 25-29, 75, 96, 201
InitialView, 60
Institute for International Education, 51, 62
Intel, 65, 141
Intellectual property 16, 30-31, 41, 48, 65-81, 83, 106, 120, 132, 155, 161
Internet, 12, 16, 25-28, 31, 39, 85, 92, 103, 116, 139, 154, 158, 159, 163, 170, 175, 194, 195
iPhones, 141

J
Ji, Chaoqun 48, 91-93
Jiang, Bo, 54
Jing, Ma, 110
Jones Day, 139

K
Kakutani, Michiko, 195
Keiretsu, 149
Kennedy, Scott, 68, 105, 137-139, 163-166, 175-177
Kim, Jung-Un 30
Kissinger, Henry, 135
Knight, Phil, 181
Kolion Technology, 89, 90
Kounalakis, Markos, 109-110

L
Legendary Entertainment, 111, 114

Lenovo, 72
Leviathan, 95
Lewis & Bockius, 139
Li, Kexin, 132
Li, Shuyu, 54
Li, Yuan, 65-66, 104, 154
Lieu, Rep. Ted, 53
Link, Perry, 114-118
Lithium ion batteries, 69-71, 166
Litinsky, James, 171-174
Liu, Xiaobo, 124
Lloyd-Damnjanovic, Anastasia, 121
Lockheed Martin, 25-26
Lord, Winston, 134

M
Macquarie University, 125
Made in China 2025 program, 16, 26, 44, 72, 73, 106, 142, 150, 204
Malware, 28, 29, 33-36, 43, 44, 195
Managed Service Providers (MSPs), 33-35
Mancini, Steve, 41-42, 64, 154
Mandarin Chinese language, 8, 39, 49, 50, 60, 65, 120, 191
Mao Tse-tung, 13, 139
Marriott Hotels, 18, 97
Massachusetts Institute of Technology (MIT), 46, 69
McCarthy, Sen. Joseph, 12,

133, 193
McCartney, Robert, 43
McKinsey & Co., 85, 103
Medtronic PLC., 46
Meng, Wanzhou, 139
Mercury Public Affairs, 137
MGM Studios, 112
Micron Technology, 47, 55-
56
Microsoft, 33
Military Accessions Vital to
the National Interest
program, 93
Ministry of State Security
(China); coordinating
hacking attacks, 16;
connection to APT10
hacking group, 32; list of
technologies being
targeted, 45-46; arrest of
Yanjun Xu in GE Aviation
case, 48-52; recruiting of
Chinese students in the
United States, 62; possible
relationship with Chinese
venture capitalists, 81;
Joey Chun case, 90-91;
effort to penetrate U.S.
Army, 92-93; connections
to United Front strategy,
132; U.S. agencies show
improvement in being able
to arrest Xu, 97;
dismantling CIA network
in China, 97-98;
connection to Marriott

hack; 98; GE working
with FBI to arrest Xu a
hopeful sign, 160;
characteristics of Chinese
recruited by MSS, 192.
Morgan, Lewis, & Brockius,
139
Moser, Harry C., 182-185
Motorola, 70
Mountain Pass mine, 171-
174, 186
Myers, Steven Lee, 99

N
Nanjing University of
Aeronautics and
Astronautics, 49
Nathan, Andrew J., 116-123,
135
National Association for
China's Peaceful
Unification, 131-132
National Aviation and Space
Administration (NASA),
39, 54, 63, 164, 172
National Institutes of Health
(NIH), 67-68, 162, 175,
190, 202
National Post of Canada, 133
National Science Foundation
(NSF), 164, 175
National Security Agency
(NSA), 97
National Security Council
(NSC), 39, 44, 95, 100,
153, 159
Naval War College, 195

Navigant Consulting, 36
NBC, 110
New York Times, 9, 68, 99,
    108-110, 137, 144, 154,
    190, 195
New York University, 123-
    125
Nichols, Tom, 195
Nixon, Former President
    Richard M., 163, 167
North American Free Trade
    Agreement (NAFTA),
    163, 175
North Korea, 30, 137, 149,
    196
Northrup Grumman, 26

O
Obama, former President
    Barack, hacking agreement
    with President Xi, 27-30,
    33-38; A123 Systems, 69-
    71; efforts to streamline
    government email systems,
    153; use of Office of
    Science and Technology
    Policy, 166; possible
    mistakes made in solar
    power industry, 170;
    support for German-style
    apprentice programs, 185;
    pivot to Asia, 191.
Office of Personnel
    Management, 18, 99
Overseas Press Club and
    Overseas Press Club
    Foundation, 8-9, 15, 61

P
Pearl Harbor, 102.
Pence, Vice President Mike,
    19, 140.
People's Daily, 144, 190.
People's Liberation Army
    (PLA), 25-28, 32, 37-40,
    50, 95, 114, 152
Politico, 63
Porter, Christopher, 29-35,
    100, 157-158, 168
Priestap, E.W., 65

Q
Qin, Amy, 112
Qiu, Zhongsun 130-131
Qualcomm 70, 137, 142,
    167

R
Research & Development
    (R&D), 16, 42, 46, 66-67,
    86, 160, 168, 175-177,
    203
Radio Free Asia, 130
Raytheon, 26
Reagan, former President
    Ronald, 78
Rhodium Group, 72
Robotics 51, 63, 75-78, 82,
    162, 167, 170
Rosenstein, Rod J., 32-35
Royce, Ed, 138
Rubio, Sen. Marco, 138, 155,
    165

Russia Today, 109
Ryan, Paul, 197

S
San Francisco State
  University, 123
Sanger, David, 99
Schell, Orville, 103, 113,
  119, 135, 193
Scissors, Derek, 150
Sematech, 163, 167, 175
Seton Hill University, 41, 64
Shah, Raj, 78-79
Shambaugh, David, 135
Siddiqui, Faiz, 43
Silicon Valley, 16, 20, 42-47,
  65-86
Slaughter, Matthew J., 62
SoftBank, 77
Solyndra, 70-71, 175
Southern Avionics, 74
Spencer, Richard, 95
Sputnik, 102, 163-164
Stanford University, 39, 108,
  119
State University of New
  York, 179
State-owned enterprises
  (SOEs), 76
STEM skills, (Science,
  Technology, Engineering
  and Math), 51, 62, 80,
  122, 195
Sun Tzu and The Art of War,
  10, 20, 88, 94, 107
Super Micro Computer, Inc.,

38-39
Sweeney, William F. Jr., 91
Symantec, 79

T
T-Mobile, 57-59
Tan, Joy, 139-140
Tang, Rose, 127-134
Teledyne Technologies, 73
Temp.Periscope, 95
Tesla Motors, 66-71, 173,
  177
Texas A&M, 119
Thousand Talent Program,
  64-68
Tiananmen Square, 14, 116-
  128
Trump, President Donald J.:
  so-called trade war 11, 15,
  104, 137-142, 150;
  suggesting Des Moines
  newspaper was used for
  propaganda, 19, 108;
  interpretation of Obama-
  Xi agreement, 35; remark
  that every Chinese student
  was a spy, 62-63; ZTE
  battle, 137-139; attitude
  toward Wall Street, 153;
  effort to streamline federal
  email systems, 162;
  restrictions on Chinese
  students, 164; promoting
  AI research, 164; attitude
  toward science, 166;
  retreating on electric cars,

177; German apprentice programs, 185; call with FoxConn's Terry Gou, 186; book by Michiko Kakutani, 195

Tung, C.H., 103

Twitter 9, 130-131, 194

U

United Front Work Department and International Liaison Department, 133

United Microelectronics, 47, 56

U.S.-China Economic and Security Review Commission, 63, 77, 154, 191

U.S. Merit Systems Protection Board, 53

U.S. Trade Representative's Office, 72-75

U.S. Treasury Department, 77, 137

United States: world order established after World War II, 15; stealing steam engine technology from Britain; 17; China as the largest challenge since World War II, 18; population disadvantage, 19; China's recruitment inside, 27; Chinese advantages over, 30; origins of computer equipment, 41-42; technological culture and costs of theft; 46; recruitment on U.S. soil, 51; visa policies, 63; Chinese investment in, 72-73; venture capital investments in, 77-85; Chinese research in U.S. labs, 86; China projecting media power in, 104-113; China seeking to influence academic freedom in; 116-126; Chinese government efforts to control Chinese in U.S.; 127-135; China using systems of Western democracies to undermine them; 144; need for rare earths; 172-173; electric car industry, 176-177; ideological logjam, 177; attracting investment from U.S. companies back from abroad, 181-185; need to re-establish consumer electronics sector, 185-186.

White House 30, 39, 43, 110, 137, 145, 155, 172, 190; Office of Science and Technology Policy (OSTP), 165-166, 201

U

United Turbine, 74
University of California at Berkeley, 63, 123
University of California at San Diego, 123-124, 130, 193
University of Florida, 169
University of Georgia, 130
University of Maryland, 63, 124, 129
University of Oklahoma, 166

V
Velodyne LiDAR, 84
Verizon, 153-154
Vieau, David, 69-71, 164-171
Virtual Reality, 82
Viruses, 29, 37, 195
Vogel, Ezra, 135
Voice of America, 111

W
Wall Street Journal, 35, 47, 62-65, 94-96, 108
Wal-Mart, 141-142
Wang, An, 46, 134
Wanxiang Group Corp., 70-72
Warner, Sen. Mark R., 155, 165
Washington Post, 43, 108, 140, 144
Wayne State University, 68
WeChat, 131
Wessel, Michael, 63

West, Darrell W., 141
Westlake Capital, 79
Wilson, Roy 68
Wilson Center, 121-122, 192
Worden, Minky, 51, 118-125, 144
Wray, Christopher, 32-36, 66, 189-190

X
Xi, President Jinping: broad policies, 8, 12, 15-16, 135, 150, 189; rallying nation, 13; new world order, 18; Chinese name styles, 21; agreement with President Obama, 27-36; pattern of Chinese acquisitions shifting, 72; One Belt, One Road initiative, 104; decision to extend his term in office, 106, 140; Made in China, 2025, program, 106; development of CGTN, 111; banning critical foreign-made movies, 112; urging CGTN to "tell China stories well", 123; making call to President Trump regarding ZTE, 137-139
Xi, Xiaoxing, 54
Xiang, Bing, 104
Xiaopeng Motors, 66
Xinhua News Agency, 109-110

Xu, Yanjun, 48-50, 92, 97,
   159

Y
Yam, Kimberly, 53-54
Yang, Shuping, 129
Ye, Tianchun, 65
Youssefzadeh, Emil, 85-86

Z
Z-Park, 66
Zhang, Shilong, 32
Zhao, Yumin, 106-107
Zheng, Xiaoqing, 45, 52
Zhu, Hua, 32
Zou, Daniel, 47
ZTE, 137-139, 153-154, 201
Zuckerberg, Mark, 157

www.ingramcontent.com/pod-product-compliance
Lightning Source LLC
Chambersburg PA
CBHW071955260326
41914CB00004B/808